D0312727

A grenade explodes (Scene Three)

Gentlemen, it works (Scene Eight)

Fifty cent for coke! (Scene Five)

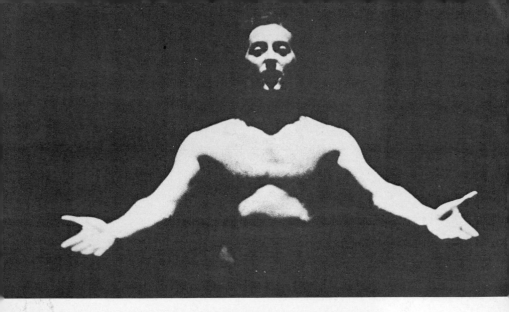

"I ain't killing MacGreever just to grease some fucking
Lieutenant Colonel . . . Me either" (Scene Ten)

Bosum and the carnage of victory (Scene Nine)

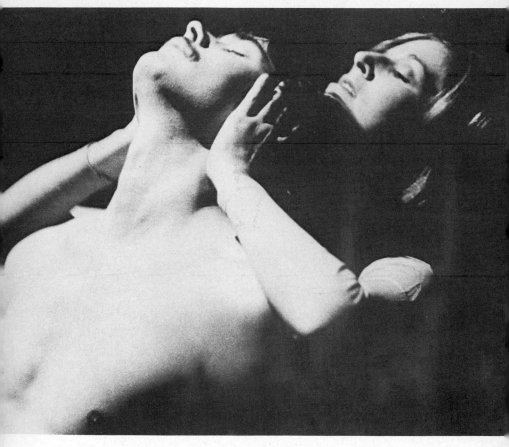

"Inside the head": Dr. Edwards listens to instructions
on body-escort duties (Scene Twelve)

Dr. Edwards remembers his conversation
with the cab driver (Scene Twelve)

David about to die (Scene Twelve)

The Dramatization of 365 DAYS

The Dramatization of

365 Days

H. WESLEY BALK

**Based
on the book
by Ronald J. Glasser, M.D.**

University of Minnesota Press, Minneapolis

Published by arrangement with George Braziller, Inc.,
publisher of the original *365 Days* by Ronald J. Glasser.
Copyright © 1971 by Ronald J. Glasser.
The Dramatization of 365 Days by H. Wesley Balk.
Copyright © 1972 by the University of Minnesota.
All rights reserved.

Printed in the United States of America
at Jones Press, Minneapolis. Published
in the United Kingdom and India by the Oxford University
Press, London and Delhi, and in Canada
by the Copp Clark Publishing Co. Limited, Toronto

Library of Congress Catalog Card Number: 72-85756

ISBN 0-8166-0670-6

Applications for permission to present the dramatization in
this volume must be made to Jerome E. Wexler, 100 North
La Salle Street, Suite 1600, Chicago, Illinois 60602. No
performance, amateur or professional, may take place unless
permission has first been obtained.

To my wife for the idea;
to Ron for taking the chance;
to Ken and Merle for their flexibility;
to Kathy, Donna, Janice, Sheriden,
Mary Ann, Peter, Doug, Fred,
Clay, Bert, Joe, Scott, Sonny, Mike,
and Tom for sweating it out.

Foreword

When I was asked to write a foreword for this book, the invitation seemed little more than a courtesy. This text is for performance in the theater, and I have absolutely no expertise in theater. Nor did I have anything to do with Wesley's dramatization of the book. When he first called to ask if he could dramatize 365 Days, I said yes, but from the very beginning I stayed out of it. I did not advise him on the editing, nor did I attend any rehearsals. This was partly because of my ever-increasing duties at the hospital but also because I was convinced that he was doomed to failure and I wanted no part of his blunder. I simply could not see how a dramatization would be effective.

I was wrong. The night that I saw the play I sat there, like everyone else, with tears streaming down my face, so distressed that I could not go home. I'd forgotten what it had been like.

When I had the courage I thanked Wesley for what he had done, not only for me but for all those boys who weren't there — and never would be.

Ronald J. Glasser, M.D.

Minneapolis, Minnesota
June 1972

vii

Contents

An Experiment in Chamber Theater

An Experiment
in Chamber Theater

by H. WESLEY BALK

On November 9, 1971, students of the University of Minnesota
Theatre Department presented a dramatization of Dr. Ronald
Glasser's book *365 Days* in the Shevlin Arena Theater. On
December 6 the University Theatre staff voted to enter the production in the American College Theater Festival. After two
preliminary performances at the Walker Art Center in Minneapolis on January 21 and 22, the production moved to the Crawford Livingston Theater in St. Paul for the Regional Competition
on February 7. The festival judges (Henry Hewes of the *Saturday
Review,* Tunc Yalman formerly of the Milwaukee Repertory
Theater, and Dan Bly of the Guthrie Theater) selected it as the
regional representative to be performed in the Kennedy Center
Eisenhower Theater in Washington, D.C., on April 24. In the
interim it was performed at Normandale State Junior College as
part of a series of seminars on the effects of the Vietnam War.
During the last week of March the University of Minnesota Press
inquired about the possibility of publishing the dramatization in
book form. Dr. Glasser and his publishers agreed, and the present
volume is the result.

In retrospect all of this sounds carefully planned and logical,
but it really began as an essay in serendipity. The production I
had planned to direct was *The Shakespeare Game,* an experiment

3

with game theory and the works of Shakespeare, a first attempt at which had excited and infuriated audiences the year before, and which I wanted to test in a different environment with different rules. But it didn't feel right. While the students were willing, they were eager to work further with chamber theater, another experimental form I had used that summer in dramatizing Jerzy Kosinski's novel *The Painted Bird*.

It was already Labor Day weekend, and *The Shakespeare Game* was listed in the University Theatre publicity releases. I drove back to Minneapolis from an opera-directing stint in Kansas City, thinking fruitlessly all the while. A midnight Saturday supper followed by the Sunday morning ritual of reading the papers in bed does not ordinarily lead to much of anything except anxiety, but that morning my wife handed me a section of the paper pointing to a review of a book called *365 Days*. It sounded powerful and relevant and seemed to make an important statement about the war. My decision was immediate: the next morning I would buy a copy of the book, I would let it fall open at random, and if the page thus revealed seemed susceptible to chamber theater treatment, I would produce *365 Days* instead of *The Shakespeare Game*. Monday arrived, I bought the book and let it fall open. The first words I read were "Final Pathological Diagnosis," and that chapter has remained for me the most powerful part of the book. Later that day I learned that Dr. Ronald Glasser lived in Minneapolis, and that we had previously met through the offices of a mutual friend who not only had designed many operas for me but had also designed the jacket for *365 Days*. Further, Dr. Glasser went along with my idea, and so did his publishers. Others may take such omens lightly. For me they only confirmed the rightness of my decision: whatever administrative hassles it might cause at the university, the book had to be done. I am most grateful that the University Theatre administrative staff agreed with me.

The definition of chamber theater is simple enough: it is theater which uses literature not written for the stage and presents it,

4

abridged but not rewritten, in theatrical form. It has various theatrical cousins such as story theater, readers' theater, and factual theater, and like them it is another attempt to find new combinations of the words-action-music blend which is part of all theater. All of these offshoots from standard dramatic form have one thing in common: they place less stress on the playwright's contribution of situation, dialogue, and characterization, emphasizing instead the performing talents actors and directors can bring to other literary forms: mime, dance-movement, choral speaking, musical use of language, musical effects of all kinds, physical metaphors and extensions of ordinary action. It is, in short, a strongly theatrical form, and if I call attention too often to the director's responsibility in finding his own answers for the dramatization of *365 Days,* it is because of the nature of the form. A traditional play contains a great deal more of the necessary verbal information needed to produce it than does the literature employed for chamber theater. In fact, literature not written for the stage contains no help at all except by implication. If the director is gifted at choreography, or improvisatory coaching, at working musically with language, or mime coaching, any or all of these elements should be an important part of his work with chamber theater. The director of chamber theater becomes a kind of playwright, albeit with another's words, creating as he must the stylistic framework of the piece as well as all the stage directions and physical elements which are ordinarily specified by the playwright. Thus the director's total responsibility in chamber theater is far greater than it is in dealing with a standard play.

Although this responsibility is heavy, it is partially relieved if one does not presume to rewrite the words as well. And since one's primary responsibility is to preserve the tone of the original, I welcome the partial straitjacket of the original words. With rare exception I use them as they exist, letting my imagination work on the problem of "What can be done to accompany the words?" rather than "How can the words be rewritten?"

5

As to the kind of literature to be used for chamber theater, this along with the techniques to be used in presenting it is up to the individual director. In my view there is literature which defies depiction in any realistic sense either on stage or in films. It is literature of enormous power, so overwhelming in its impact that one literally cannot forget it. Works of this power are rare, but they provide the basis for my personal blend of chamber theater ingredients. *The Painted Bird* and *365 Days* both describe events which leave a resonance in one's mind that no "real" experience, cinematic or otherwise, can quite capture. Preserving this resonance and heightening it theatrically is the primary aim of chamber theater.

It was perhaps a similar feeling that led both Jerzy Kosinski and Ronald Glasser to withhold the movie rights for their books on the one hand, while accepting the possibility of a chamber theater exploration on the other. Superficially, *The Painted Bird* and *365 Days* are very different in structure and style, yet the thematic statement of the two books is almost identical. *The Painted Bird* is the story of a seven-year-old boy who is abandoned in Eastern Europe at the beginning of World War II, and whose character is formed by the hideous events which overwhelm the next five years of his life as he is shunted from village to village, from one inhuman parental figure to another. It is, by extension, the story of what happened to the young, to a whole generation, because of World War II. It would be difficult to find a more accurate statement of the theme of *365 Days*: it is, more specifically than *The Painted Bird,* a chronicle of what has happened to another generation because of another war. The fact that this war is still, tragically, absurdly, going on, and that the generation being affected is not European but American (as well, of course, as Vietnamese), gives the book a painful relevance beyond the immediate impact of the words themselves.

Equally striking is the moral commitment of the two books. Our production of *365 Days* was constantly described as "matter-

6

of-fact," "clinical," "scientifically objective," "reflective," and "understated" by the same critics who stressed the power of the production. In early rehearsals we had many heated discussions about the amount of human emotion the actors should project. We were all horrified, appalled, and outraged by turns as we encountered the material. Some of the actors felt a deep need to communicate this anger and sorrow; they felt that the objective, clinical approach was the route of timid noncommitment, that these truths should be projected with maximum intensity. It was only by returning to the book itself that the issue was resolved. Both Glasser and Kosinski obviously felt as deeply as it was possible to feel about their subject matter; yet, just as obviously, they both scrupulously avoided emotionalizing the material. The very strength of both books lies in their factual description of events rather than personal emotional reactions. We realized that our answer lay in the same approach: the avoidance of preaching, haranguing, or projecting any feelings of moral superiority. Glasser allowed his readers to draw their own conclusions; we had to do the same, presenting the material clearly, with as many tools of the theater as we could appropriately muster, with maximum energy, concentration, and precision, and let the audience make its own decisions. Of the many critics and audience members we encountered, only one missed this vital point.

So we produced Ronald Glasser's book. And now I am trying to convey some sense of that production so that others might produce it as well. At first I felt presumptuous, as if I were saying, "This is the particular editing of *365 Days* which you must use in presenting it as a theater piece," but later I realized that any director worth his salt would simply regard my specific choices as flexible guidelines to his own work in preparing the book for production. In any case, my primary interest is that as many Americans as possible see the dramatization or read the book, and if this discussion of our production leads to that end, it is worth it. Any director planning to produce the dramatization, of course,

7

should read the book itself and draw from it any additional material he desires, substituting for or adding to the text here presented. This was my relationship to the book in creating the present text and anyone else re-creating it should, I think, engage the book in the same sort of directorial dialogue, testing other excerpts and different sequences as he rehearses. My own editing, for example, was influenced by many ad hoc contingencies. We selected ninety minutes of material from more than seven hours' worth; other directors might desire more or less. We could not locate an available black actor for our production, so the dead soldier in "Final Pathological Diagnosis" was described as Caucasian instead of Negro. Similarly, I was forced to omit the Leroy Washington episode in "Gentlemen, It Works." We had also intended to dramatize the glossary, but ended by printing it in the program. Options such as these, omitted from this dramatization, can and should be considered by every director of the work.

Once the editing has been decided upon, the principal staging problem in chamber theater is finding the right "physicalization." By physicalization, I mean any action, tableau, or concerted movement which clarifies, heightens, or enlarges upon the situation described by the words. For *365 Days* many of these are suggested in the notes, but a specific example might clarify the point. In the "Medics" scene, when Graham is described as running with a triggered grenade caught in his chest webbing, the actor portraying Graham stood in place, while four of the women knelt around him, placed their hands on his waist, and began rocking him back and forth. The running thus became an undulation caused by the women. The fifth woman approached him from the front, and as the repetition of "running" by the rest of the cast reached its rhythmic peak, she struck his chest with open palms, suddenly stopping both the sound and his movement, to represent the grenade exploding. (The first photograph in the picture section captures this moment.)

For every literary experience there exists a physical realization of this general nature which will enable the audience to hear the words with greater impact than if they were simply read aloud. This at least is the article of faith with which the director should begin his work. It became evident to me as we rehearsed that the power of the text would be undercut by any sort of graphic realism, that as the literary experience became more violent or fantastic, the possibility of treating it realistically diminished. Instead we had to find visual poetry, physical metaphors (like the preceding example) which related to the experiences described but which did not simply duplicate them visually. It might be useful to take a line, not from *365 Days,* and discuss the available alternatives as opposed to the final choice described above. Take this line: "In a rage, he drove the dagger into her breast." The line might be accompanied physically in any of the following ways. A man approaches a woman, speaks the line gently, and kisses her on the forehead. She sinks to the floor and kneels at his feet. Or the man touches the woman in four places as he speaks the line, she contorting her body at each touch. Or the woman speaks the line and draws the man toward her, manipulating his actions, implying the idea of suicide. Or two other people manipulate the man and woman physically while a third person speaks the line. If the two manipulators were other characters in the story, it would be implied that they caused the murder. Further alternatives could be described, but the possibilities are evident. The choice depends, once again, on the taste of the director, the talent of his cast, and the meaning of the piece of literature as the director and his cast see it. Our physical choices for *365 Days* were spare, austere, highly disciplined, and explosive in their transitions. The kind of ritual that resulted was not achieved by aiming for ritual from the beginning, but rather from the searching process of rehearsal, and from the stripping down of emotional indulgence, clever choreography, overly imaginative mime, and vocal pyrotechnics.

Although the text for *365 Days* was not rewritten, there were a number of technical additions and rearrangements made for the purposes of dramatization. In "Bosum," for example, commands such as "Forward march!" were added. Occasional changes in person or tense were also made: "He began to unwrap the gauze from around the patient's head" became "Edwards unwrapped the gauze from around the patient's head." Group cries of various kinds and other nonverbal sounds were also employed. Whatever was done, one thing came to seem more and more important: the flow of sound, whether words, music, or simply nonverbal cries, had to be almost continuous. There were, of course, occasional pauses but these were carefully planned as part of the musical continuum. The discipline this demands from a cast is immense. The usual motivational or character cues which assist an actor in memorization simply do not exist in chamber theater to the extent they do in more traditional plays. For example, there is no reason why Speaker 6 and Speaker 8 should say, "Technically they're right" and "Once the chopper picks you up" in that order even though that was the actual assignment of lines. Combine this kind of mental effort with strenuous physical tasks and you are asking your actors for a monumental expenditure of energy.

Beyond the problem of sheer mental and physical energy lies that of the actor's attitude, previously discussed. As we worked, I came to realize that what we were trying to achieve was closer to the idea of Brechtian acting than anything I had encountered in actually working with Brecht's plays. We were trying to say "This is what happened" as clearly and precisely as possible and not "This is what is happening" in realistic emotional terms. This meant the actors could and should take an attitude about what *had* happened rather than expressing the attitude of a person to whom it was *happening*. One critic pointed out an interesting example of this: "When the doctor describes his experience with the wounded by saying, 'It's sort of clean work. No brain tumors to worry about, no chronic renal disease, no endless dialysis, no multiple sclerosis, no leukemia — and no goddamn families to have to worry about,' the lines emerge with a soft, sad irony

10

rather than with cynicism. This is valuable, for if we believed the doctor-author to be cynical, a strong point of view might have been transmitted, but the play might not have remained a beautifully unbiased work to which the audience can make its own response." In Brechtian terms, the actor was adding his own comment to the lines rather than simply playing the cynicism of the character who said them. This is a more complex, multilayered approach than straight naturalism affords, and is especially useful in chamber theater. There was no way we could scream the scream which echoes through the book any more than we could physicalize the carnage which caused the scream. And even though characterization was clearly called for in certain scenes, the most important thing was the precisely timed, highly energized delivery of information which the audience could relate to the accompanying physical metaphors. This does not mean that the delivery should be mechanical or computerlike, but simply that it should have great strength, economy, and directness. The young, realistically oriented actor (and very few young American actors are not) will find this difficult at first, but eventually, as was the case with our cast, the discipline becomes second nature (although always demanding great energy), and the actors are able to add more of themselves to the product.

The music for the song used in *365 Days* was composed by Tom Johnson, a brilliant young composer from Minneapolis who had written an excellent musical before he was out of high school and who has gone on from there to compose other musicals and dozens of exciting songs. He wrote six versions of the song for our dramatization, setting the opening poem in the book, and allowed the cast to choose the one which seemed the most appropriate in mood and style. (See pages 28–29.) Once the song was learned, we used it in sections throughout the piece, sometimes singing it, sometimes humming it. The guitarist, Peter Ludwig, was cast for his acting ability. It was only at the first read-through that we discovered that he played the guitar well enough not only to accom-

11

pany the song but also to create many additional musical and sound effects. The selection of similar effects must depend, as it did in our case, upon the ability of the guitar player and the desires of the director. Transitions, in particular, are terribly important in making the piece cohere, and a number of guitar effects, such as repeated, hard-driving chords, or gentle undulating rhythms, proved valuable in this respect.

Choosing a cast was very difficult and inevitably somewhat arbitrary since I was not certain at that time about the assignment of lines and the interpretation. A variety of male types was clearly needed, from teenage draftees to aging commanding officers, and we finally cast ten men: four were officer types (one of them being the guitar player), four were enlisted men or teenage "grunts," and two could swing either way. The problem with the women was different. There were no actual female character roles called for since we were not using the "Joan" chapter, but a feminine element seemed necessary to me even though its function was at first unclear. As we rehearsed, however, the role of the women was defined almost more quickly than that of the men, and their aesthetic function proved one of the central metaphors of the piece: they came to represent the passive, feminine role of the Vietnamese, as opposed to the aggressive, masculine role of the Americans, represented by the men. They also represented weapons, wounds, environmental hazards, and mental anxieties, in short, anything that acted upon the men from jungle vines to memories of home. The women thus carried a whole complex of meanings relating to the frustrations of Americans trying to fight a guerrilla-style war: the by now familiar strategy of attack and run, the ambushes, the almost seductive and sensual teasing game of hide and seek, which elicits the more deadly game of search and destroy, the unwillingness to "fight like a man out in the open," and all the indirect and subtle but seemingly more effective methods of waging this kind of war.

The importance of the sound continuum has already been discussed, and it was a strong factor in the casting as well. I looked for as wide a range of voice types as possible: low, high, rough, smooth, intense, mellifluous. When one is denied the asset of characterization and emotional attitudinizing, the basic quality and range of the voices becomes more important. The physical conditioning of the actors is also important, but we found that the sheer effort of rehearsing the piece got the actors in shape even if they were not so at the beginning.

The production began in an arena theater, moved to a modified proscenium theater, then to a thrust stage, from there to a basement gymnasium, and finally to a traditional proscenium theater. The ground plans that follow this section are based on a proscenium adaptation of the original arena staging. Had the production begun in a proscenium theater, I have no doubt that the ground plans would have looked very different from what they do. Once again, therefore, I encourage the director to regard them as departure points rather than final statements. In most cases I have selected key physicalizations to illustrate in the ground plans. Each scene involved one or two major physical arrangements which could be altered and re-formed as the scene progressed. A specific example is Ground Plan 9 in which we tried to capture the tedium of a long, meaningless, but deadly march by spreading the men out in a diamond formation. They simply moved in place, hit the floor when explosions occurred in the text, reversed directions, and continued to march in place. The pattern of march-explosion-reversal continued, there was great violence, men died one after another, but no one got anywhere — all were caught on a treadmill, randomly plucked off to die. Finally the accumulated frustration exploded in the almost ritualistic murder of a Vietnamese peasant for a coke (a My Lai in miniature).

The critical reaction to the play was interesting in that most of the critics seemed to understand both the technique and its function (a relatively rare phenomenon in my experience), and

13

for the remarkable continuity of reaction to the production as it moved from arena to thrust to proscenium. When the production opened in the Shevlin Arena Theater, the approach was described as follows in the *Minneapolis Star* for November 19, 1971:

"365 Days" . . . is a shattering experience.

It drags its audience unwillingly through the heat, mud and death of what we all know as Vietnam.

Fifteen actors, their faces whitened, clad in black combat trousers, are the only props. The 10 men are barechested. The five women wear snug, drab, grey tops.

The 15 are all the things you find in Vietnam. They are trees, waves on the Mekong River, grunts, medics, VC, gooks and death.

The script is Glasser's. The actors alternate in maintaining the narrative. They tell the stories with the same impassive outrage that marked Glasser's narrative.

Whether Balk has succeeded in surpassing the immense power of Glasser's book is unimportant. He certainly has succeeded in equaling it.

At the close of the performance . . . a woman whispered, "I can't clap."

Neither could any member of the audience. There were a few tears, the rustle of coats being pulled over shoulders, but hardly a word and not even the suggestion of applause.

Here we were grateful for the recognition of our duplication of Glasser's "impassive outrage." We felt a deep concern about accusing the audience in a condescending manner, and in a tiny arena theater this is difficult to avoid. When the play was performed on the thrust stage of the Crawford Livingston Theater, Henry Hewes said in the *Saturday Review* of February 26, 1972:

The secret of director H. Wesley Balk's approach is that, by the use of poetic movement and a non-literal miming of gruesome occurrences, we are led gently through the material. The tone is reflective, with no effort made to assault or convince the audience. And yet the drama's impact is all the more effective for the understatement. . . . The performers refrain from sarcastic inflections

14

that could have sharpened some speeches. . . . A strong point of view might have been transmitted, but the play might not have remained a beautifully unbiased work to which the audience can make its own response.

Moving from a 100-seat arena theater to a 600-seat thrust-stage theater was largely a matter of refocusing the physicalizations toward the new audience relationship. The greatest concern in all our minds was the loss of intimacy, but, as one member of the theater staff suggested, the clinical and objective tone might benefit from distancing the audience. This proved true as we performed in the Kennedy Center Eisenhower Theater in Washington, D.C., where the audience was even further removed. The *Washington Evening Star* commented on April 25, 1972:

. . . as a depiction of the human suffering in this war, it carries the impact of a dozen howitzers.
The tone is matter-of-fact, clinical, as scientifically objective as you can get when you're talking about human bodies blown past all recognition, bodies charred like firewood, bodies scarred psychically to the point of paralysis. . . . Director Balk has created a quasi-abstract choreography for his players. He has rightly recognized that the text is so potent in itself that a more graphic stage illustration would be self-defeating. The word, delivered clearly and dispassionately by the disciplined cast, does all the work.

The Washington Post, also on April 25, said:

In concept and style, the University of Minnesota returned to theater as ritual. . . . Its "365 Days" proved a moving threnody on our Vietnam dead. Its simplicity, grounded in theater's deepest roots, reflected the deepest spirit of today's youth. . . . The young bodies glide, stomp, stretch, lie and grow still across the stage. Boys in their late teens are recalled not as the individuals they must have been but for what they represented and the ghastly cruelties their bodies endured.
By avoidance of facile emotion, the truest emotion is reached and one leaves the theater more as one leaves a memorial service privately absorbed in a public place.

In spite of our doubts Ronald Glasser's words always acted upon the minds of those willing to endure the pain of listening to them whether they were two feet or forty feet from the performance. It would be absurd, of course, to imply that everyone who saw the production approved of it. But there was always a strong response, whether negative or positive, as this report on the final performance in Washington indicates (*Washington Sunday Star,* April 30, 1972):

. . . it is the word, unadorned and unassisted, that unrolls the ghastly tapestry before our eyes and asks us to come to grips with its truth. What is the effect?

Judging from Monday's performance, it is multiple. There were indignant walkouts, perhaps as upset by some of the scatological epithets as they were by the actual subject matter. (Those who walked out were, incidentally, castigated with boos by a portion of the audience.) There were audible gasps of terror at the description of a soldier's body deprived in death of the most remote human proportions. A middle-aged gentleman before me murmured angrily that he knew someone who knew someone in Nixon's office, and dammit, the President was going to hear about this foolishness. And there was another middle-aged man across the way who sputtered that "people like that should be chained to their seats and made to watch the play three times." In short, there was tangible response — response in the theater where polite applause and muffled yawns are the exhausted coinage with which our actors are usually paid. And in that plush red lobby, after it was over, there was the numbed quiet that overtakes an audience, touched in those depths beyond reason.

One man was heard to remark, "That language isn't fit for the ears of my wife!" whereupon a woman replied, "Then she obviously hasn't visited a ladies' room recently." It is always shocking that people will respond with greater outrage to a spoken word like "fuck" than they will to the far more obscene events being portrayed at the same time. There is surely some relationship between the reluctance of segments of our public

16

to accept the reality of the common language-as-spoken by their own sons in the army and our national reluctance to face the reality of the United States' position in Vietnam.

As is evident from the foregoing the performance was not an entertainment. It was stark and austere and ultimately exhausting. There was no intermission, there was no relief. One saw the dead lying there when entering the theater; the dead were the last thing one saw when the theater emptied. The performance became for everyone involved a kind of sacramental act, a ritual performed in order that the events it represented might be purged from the realm of the necessary. It began with the word, and in the end the word remained, cradled in the ritual it had created, so that all who heard it, in the words of Dr. Glasser, "knew it, even if they didn't like it, they knew it."

Ground Plans and Song

Ground plans drawn by M. E. Gramatky

ALL NUMBERS REFER TO SPEAKERS
⊗ MEN
⊙ WOMEN
○—< RECUMBENT

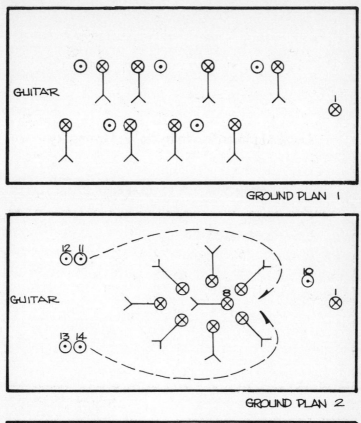

GUITAR

GROUND PLAN 1

GUITAR

GROUND PLAN 2

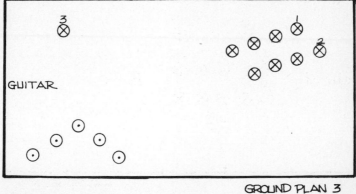

GUITAR

GROUND PLAN 3

21

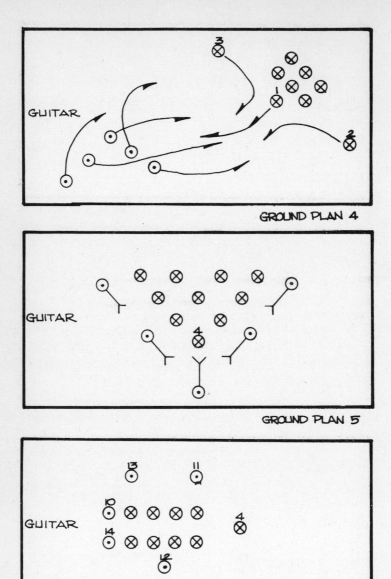

GUITAR

GROUND PLAN 4

GUITAR

GROUND PLAN 5

GUITAR

GROUND PLAN 6

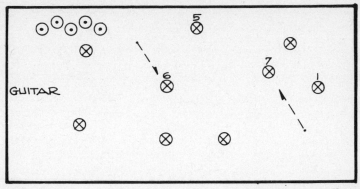

GROUND PLAN 7

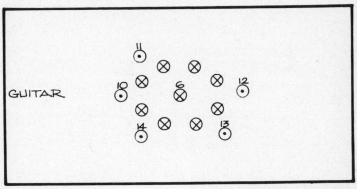

GROUND PLAN 8

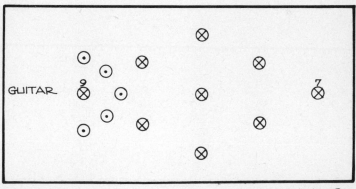

GROUND PLAN 9

23

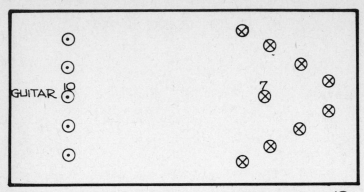

GROUND PLAN 10

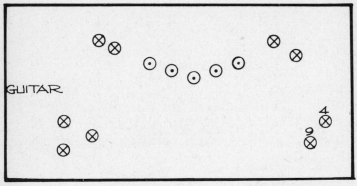

GROUND PLAN 11

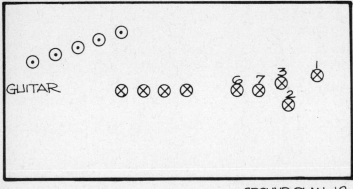

GROUND PLAN 12

24

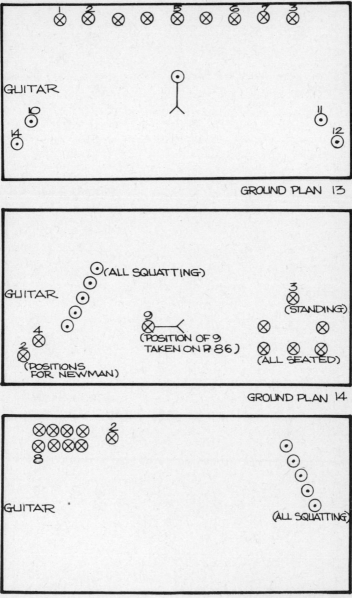

GUITAR

GROUND PLAN 13

(ALL SQUATTING)

GUITAR

3
(STANDING)

9
(POSITION OF 9
TAKEN ON P.86)

4

2
(POSITIONS
FOR NEWMAN)

(ALL SEATED)

GROUND PLAN 14

2

8

GUITAR

(ALL SQUATTING)

GROUND PLAN 15

25

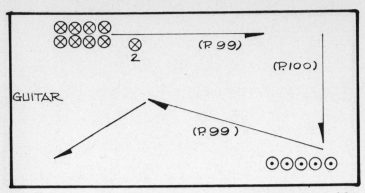

GROUND PLAN 16

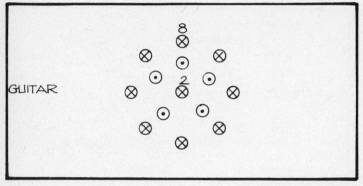

GROUND PLAN 17

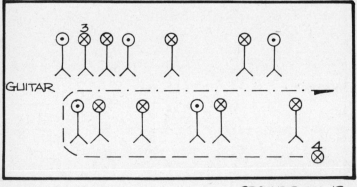

GROUND PLAN 18

26

GUITAR

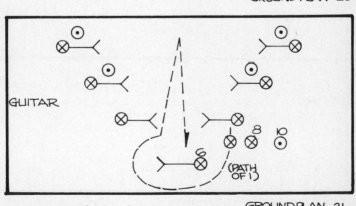

GUITAR

(MEN SEATED LEGS STRAIGHT)

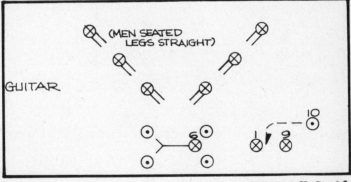

GUITAR

(PATH OF 1)

365 Days

28

boy   it's the A- mer-'i- 'can   way

CHORUS) G₇

We hav-en't de-cid-ed you're wrong for ex-pe-ri-ence has its

func - tion   But my mind is at the cross-roads, and I

② I can't find the junc-tion

③ * But you've thrown us out here on the back roads and I'm

gon-na find the junc - tion

29

The Dramatization

The dramatization of *365 Days* was first performed on November 9, 1971, in the Shevlin Arena Theater of the University of Minnesota.

Production Staff

Director	H. WESLEY BALK
Stage manager	RICHARD SMITH (Shevlin Arena performance)
	MARY KAY TESSMAN (other performances)
Lighting design	RICHARD SMITH (Shevlin Arena performance)
	MARY KAY TESSMAN (other performances)
Costume design	ROBIN REID
Makeup design	SHERIDEN THOMAS
Technical direction	RICHARD SEIFERT, JEAN MONTGOMERY

Cast

Guitarist	PETER LUDWIG
Speaker 1	DOUGLAS HAMILTON
Speaker 2	FRED THOMPSON
Speaker 3	CLAYTON BERRY
Speaker 4	WILBERTO ROSARIO
Speaker 5	JOSEPH RASSULO
Speaker 6	SCOTT CLELAND
Speaker 7	SONNY LINDNER
Speaker 8	MICHAEL BOYLE
Speaker 9	THOMAS MILLER
Speaker 10	KATHY LENEL
Speaker 11	DONNA HALEY
Speaker 12	JANICE ROBILLARD
Speaker 13	SHERIDEN THOMAS
Speaker 14	MARY ANN LIPPAY

365 Days

Scene One: Zama

As the audience enters, the cast is seen lying on the stage in two rows to suggest death, a cemetery, a morgue. When the performance is ready to begin, the guitarist — who remains in his position, on a stool, unless otherwise specified — plays a chord and the cast rises slowly to form a large circle. A second chord is then struck and the cast squats down, as though around a large campfire. They sing the first verse of their song in this position, then rise as they sing the second verse to face the audience in two ranks, like soldiers. As the third verse is concluding, the men lie down in place, to suggest hospital beds, with Speaker 1 standing at the left and the women standing above the men like nurses. See Ground Plan 1. In the first production, in the round, the cast marched in very slowly, like a death march, rather than being discovered on stage.

Cast

  Tonight I'm with myself again
  I'm talking with my mind
  These last three months we've talked a lot
  And found we're in a bind

  Not that we're different
  We don't think we're unique

33

But the answers that we're questioning
Are those we've heard you speak

We haven't decided you're wrong
For experience has a function
But my mind is at the crossroad
And I think I'm at a junction

Speaker 1

These pages were not written in desperation, nor were they written out of boredom, or even, I think, to prove a point, but rather to offset the sinking feeling we all had that some day, when the whole thing was over, there would be nothing remembered except the confusion and the politics. There is, of course, something else to be remembered. (*As Speaker 1 walks from stage left to stage right between the two rows, the women move slowly from body to body, finally kneeling down by them. Speaker 1 returns to the stage left end.*) There was a time the Army hospitals in Japan, to one of which I was assigned, were averaging six to eight thousand patients a month. (During the Tet offensive it had been closer to eleven.) The surgeons seemed ready for the emergency, and even the internists. But I had been sent to Japan as a pediatrician to serve the children of the dependent military population there. (*The women raise the men slowly so that they are seated, their legs straight out in front of them on the floor. The women move from man to man until they have raised them all, and then stand over them, waiting.*) I soon realized that the troopers they were pulling off those med evac choppers were only children themselves.

Speaker 11

Loss is a part of pediatrics.

Speaker 12

Two infants in four thousand are born with a severe congenital anomaly.

Speaker 13

Fifteen percent of all prematures are mentally retarded.

Speaker 14

One out of twenty thousand children will get leukemia.

Speaker 10

The rest you struggle over: the meningitises, the pneumonias, the poisonings, and the accidents.

Speaker 11

They set the tone, for to save one child is to save the whole thing. (*One by one, the women suddenly, explosively, but quietly pounce upon the men over whom they have been standing, and twist and bend their bodies and heads. They move to other men and repeat the process until all have been touched.*)

Speaker 1

But to save him only to see him blown apart or blinded, to help him grow properly only to have his spinal cord transected, or to have him burned to death, puts all the effort in doubt; the vaccines, the pediatric research, the new techniques, and the endless concern — suddenly it all seemed so foolish, so hopeless. To lose a child, at any time along his life, is really to lose the whole thing. (*The guitarist plays a cuttingly clear dissonant chord. The women move very briskly from man to man in random patterns, as though they were nurses in a very busy hospital, finally kneeling once again at the heads of the men. Quiet, flowing dissonant fingerpicking of the guitar underscores the lines from "Zama . . ." to "not stop screaming," with the harmonics used as quiet, yet staccato, underlinings of "the blind seventeen-year-olds" and "the shattered high-school football player."*) Zama, where I was assigned in September 1968, was a 700-bed hospital with a small pediatric unit of five beds and a nursery. It was the only general Army hospital in Japan. There is not, I think, a community in America that would not have been proud and happy to have had our hospital, just as it was, serving it. Literally thousands of boys were saved. But the effort had its price; after a while it all began

35

to seem so natural; even the blind seventeen-year-olds stumbling down the hallway, or the shattered high-school football player being wheeled to physical therapy. At first, I was glad I didn't know them; I was relieved they were your children, not mine. After a while, I changed. These kids were so brave, they endured so much, they were so uncomplaining that you couldn't help but feel proud of them. (*The guitarist has been playing a soft two-note pattern which increases in volume. The men slowly open their mouths and put their heads back as in a silent scream. The action peaks with the guitar as Speaker 1 says "screaming."*) I can remember only one boy who would not stop screaming. (*pause until the guitar stops*) In the beginning I talked with them just to have something to say and to get them talking. Later I came to realize they were all saying the same things — without quite saying them. (*Gently, one by one, the women speak their lines and reach out to the men, caressing their faces and cradling their heads. Dissonant variations of a guitar chord should underlie the next five speeches, ending in a heavy strum accenting "love them when they got back."*)

Speaker 11

They were worried, every one of them, not about the big things, not about survival, but about how they would explain away their lost legs or the weakness in their right arms.

Speaker 12

Would they embarrass their families?

Speaker 13

Would they be able to make it at parties where guys were still whole?

Speaker 14

Could they go to the beach and would their scars darken in the sun and offend the girls?

Speaker 10

Would they be able to get special cars? Above all, and underlining all their cares, would anybody love them when they got back?

36

(*The women rise and slowly move among the men, finally stand-ing between them in ranks once again.*)

Speaker 1

The stories I have tried to tell here are true. I would have liked to disbelieve some of them, and at first I did, but I was there long enough to hear the same stories again and again, and then to see part of it myself. If there is more to say it will have to be said by others, though I wonder how they will do it. There is no novel in Nam, there is not enough for a plot, nor is there really any character development. If you survive 365 days without getting killed or wounded you simply go home and take up again where you left off. (*The guitar accents the line with a dry, resigned chord, unmuted.*) As for me, my wish is not that I had never been in the Army, but that this book could never have been written. (*The men rise rapidly with an explosive, staccato cry and face the audience, once again in two ranks.*)

Men

(*like soldiers in ranks "sounding off" they repeat in rapid succes-sion*) Why write?

Speaker 7

Why write anything? Who wants to be reminded?

Speaker 8

There are no veterans' clubs for this war, no unit reunions, no pictures on the walls.

Speaker 5

For those who haven't been there, or are too old to go, it's as if it doesn't count.

Speaker 7

For those who've been there, and managed to get out, it's like it never happened.

Speaker 9

Only the eighteen-, nineteen-, and twenty-year-olds have to worry, and since no one listens to them, it doesn't matter.

37

Guitarist

But there were 6000 patients evac'ed to Japan last month. (*The women move briskly from man to man as though marking numerals on their chests.*) You'd think that so many wounded would be hard to ignore, but somehow, as Peterson says, they're written off each month — a wastage rate . . .

Speaker 1

(*overlapping*) . . . a wastage rate — a series of contrapuntal numbers, which seems to make it all not only acceptable, but strangely palatable as well.

Guitarist

(*overlapping*) . . . palatable as well. Perhaps Peterson's right. And if he is, then everything is a bit closer to what Herbert said when he woke up in the recovery room and found they'd taken off his leg.

Men

Fuck you! (*The cry of "Fuck you!" — like "Why write?" — is delivered in rapid succession by all the men.*)

Speaker 4

Fuck you one and all. (*Another explosive cry by the men as all but Speaker 2 hit the ground. He remains standing, along with the women, who stalk among the men, ready to pounce.*)

Speaker 2

The Army likes to pride itself that no one hit in Nam is more than ten minutes away from the nearest hospital. (*Speaker 2 hits the ground as though avoiding an explosion.*)

Speaker 6

Technically, they're right. (*As each man raises his head to speak his line, the women move as though to attack him. When the line is concluded, the man lowers his head sharply.*)

Speaker 8

Once the chopper picks you up, it's a ten-minute ride to the nearest surg or evac facility . . .

Speaker 3

. . . maybe a bit longer if you're really lit up . . .

Speaker 5

. . . and the med evac has to overfly the nearest small hospital and go on to the closest evac.

Speaker 7

But the choppers still have to get in and get the troopers out.

Speaker 9

By this time, over 4000 choppers will have been shot down.

Speaker 11

An RPD round travels at 3000 feet per second. (*As each woman speaks, she drops rapidly on one of the men, not touching him, but holding herself just above him with her arms, speaking the information sensuously but rapidly into his head. The men hug the floors.*)

Speaker 12

A 200-pound chicon mine can turn over a 20-ton personnel carrier.

Speaker 13

A buried 105-mm shell can blow an engine block through the cab of a truck.

Speaker 14

A claymore sends out between 200 and 400 ball bearings at the speed of 1000 feet per second.

Speaker 10

For the VC and NVA it's a close-up war.

Speaker 11

There is nothing very indiscriminate about their killings — booby traps and small arms, ten meters — and they're looking at you all the time. (*The women rise quickly and move stage right. All the men except Speaker 1 make a hissing sound and rapidly form a circle around Speaker 8, stretching out on the floor to do so. The women move stage left around the men. Speaker 12 then moves into the circle from the stage left side — see Ground Plan 2 —*

and raises Speaker 8 to a sitting position as she speaks her line.
Speakers 13 and 14 follow her and lower themselves on either
side of Speaker 8, placing their heads on his shoulder. Speaker
11 follows and lowers herself directly onto Speaker 8, in push-up
position, as Speaker 10, who remains standing, says "As he
fell back . . .")

Speaker 1

We had a patient shot through the chest. He was in his hutch
when he thought he heard something moving outside.

Speaker 12

The moonlight came in through the door, cutting a path of light
across the floor. Sitting up put him in it.

Speaker 13

The gook was waiting, lying on the ground, no more than two
meters from the door.

Speaker 14

He let off a single round that ripped through the trooper's chest.

Speaker 10

As he fell back the VC put his weapon on automatic and shot the
shit out of the rest of the hutch.

Guitarist

If you're going to die in Nam, you'll die straight out, right where
it happens. (*As the guitarist speaks, the women move slowly to
form a line across the back of the stage. The men move again into
two ranks facing the audience and lie down as before.*)

Speaker 1

If you don't die right out you've got a pretty good chance. If the
wounded get to Japan, the survival rate is an astonishing ninety-
eight percent.

Guitarist

Part of it is the medical care and the facilities in Nam — the
incredibly fine care and dedication that go into it. But mostly
it's the kind of war we're fighting. (*During the following speeches,
the women move briskly, mechanically, between the bodies,*

executing sharp right and left turns, as though super-efficient nurses. By the time they conclude the rapid staccato listing of medical operations, they have moved to the down right area, where they squat and wait, facing stage left. As "Enucleations" is reached, the guitarist plays a series of staccato chords during which the men move to the next formation facing Speakers 1 and 2 who are standing stage left; see Ground Plan 3.)

Speaker 11

During Tet, the 12th did seventy major cases a day — everything: Wound debridement.

Speaker 12

Vessel repairs.

Speaker 13

Tendon repairs.

Speaker 14

Abdominal explorations.

Speaker 10

Ventricular shunts.

Speaker 11

Liver resections.

Speaker 12

Nephrectomies.

Speaker 13

Burr holes.

Speaker 14

Chest tubes.

Speaker 10

Amputations.

Speaker 11

Craniotomies.

Speaker 12

Retinal repairs.

Speaker 13

Enucleations.

Speaker 2

(*as he speaks he turns the men facing him, one by one, and gives them a gentle push toward the squatting women; the women intercept the men, catching them across the body with their arms; the men crumple, in slow motion, and lie down on the floor*) Lenhardt sends every patient he can back to Nam. He's sent troopers back to the paddies with thirteen-inch thoracectomy scars and bits of claymores still in their chests. But he believes in the war and the sacrifice, in the need for making a stand and dying for it if you have to.

Speaker 1

Peterson sends everyone he can home. (*Speaker 1 turns the men lined up in front of him and gives them a gentle push toward Speaker 3. Speaker 3 stops them, turns them, and pushes them in turn toward the women, who intercept them as they did the others until, by the time Speaker 3 has finished, all the men are lying on the floor among the squatting women.*)

Speaker 3

But the Army feels differently, and so there is a pretty good chance that by feeling sorry for these kids and sending them back to the States he's killed a few. A tour in Nam for an enlisted man is not considered complete unless he has been there ten months, five days. But if you are in a medical facility, discharged and declared fit for duty, and have served a combined time, either in Nam or in a hospital, of less than ten months, five days, you go back into the computer and if the Army still needs you, you get spit back to Nam. Not for the rest of your tour, but for a complete new twelve months. It's the Army regulations. (*One by one the men rise and return to Speaker 1. They form ranks behind him and squat down as though he were protecting them.*)

Speaker 1

Peterson tries to hold them now; if they're getting close to the ten-month, five-day deadline, he'll try to extend their profiles thirty days to keep them in the hospital over the deadline. It doesn't go over very big with headquarters, but he's the Doc and you don't need a panel for a thirty-day extension of a temporary profile. You can fool around with the Army if you want and do it very effectively without having to go outside the system. (*Speaker 3 crosses to Speaker 1.*)

Speaker 3

But you have to care, really care, because the Army doesn't like to be fiddled with. (*addressing Speaker 1 directly*) I want that man out of this hospital today.

Speaker 1

He's having gastric distress, relieved by food, and there is a history of possible bleeding ulcer.

Speaker 3

I want him out, I said.

Speaker 1

It wouldn't look good for this hospital, or any of us, Colonel, to have him sent back here bleeding, especially when he left here with an impression of possible bleeding ulcer on his chart.
. . .

Speaker 3

Has anyone else seen him?

Speaker 1

No, but I don't remember anything in the Army regulations that states a physician has to get an opinion from another physician before admitting a patient to his service, do you? Of course, I could be wrong . . . (*Guitar chord. Speaker 3 does a sharp about-face and takes three steps away.*)

Guitarist

As a military physician, how you feel about the situation depends on how you look at the war — and, of course, the casualties.

Speaker 2

Lenhardt, for instance, sees nothing wrong with the war; he says it's better to fight the communists in Vietnam than in Utah. If you see the patients, broken and shattered at eighteen and nineteen,

43

as something necessary in the greater scheme of things, then there are no complaints.

Speaker 1

But if you see these kids as victims, their suffering faces, burned and scarred, their truncated stumps as personal affronts and lifelong handicaps, then you may take a chance on doing what you think is right. (*The guitarist begins the introduction to the song.*)

Scene Two: Mayfield

The men begin a slow march from upstage left to downstage right as they begin singing. Speakers 2 and 3 join them. As they do so, the women rise and begin moving in and out of the marching ranks of men. (See Ground Plan 4.) Only the men sing the first verse, and as the women join them on the second verse, they freeze in midstep. Only the women sing "You owe it to your country, boy, It's the American Way," each of them speaking to one of the men. As the third verse begins, the men break ranks slowly and fill the stage in a random pattern.

Cast

You sent us here to join you
And to fight your distant war
We did, but even those who make it home
Carry back a scar

The answer that we question most
Is one we've heard you say,
"You owe it to your country, boy,
It's the American Way"

We haven't decided you're really wrong
For experience has its function
But my mind is at the crossroad

(The guitar abruptly interrupts the song with a staccato explosion. All the men hit the floor. The women move upstage, forming a line across the back.)

Speaker 4

Mayfield lay in the water, listening. He was tired. Not exhausted, just tired out.

Speaker 11

A single round cracked out from the tree line, but nobody bothered to fire back. *(accented with a crisp harmonic note from the guitar)*

Speaker 4

Closing his eyes, he tried to relax.

Speaker 9

They're coming, Sarge.

Speaker 4

I know.

Speaker 12

A few moments later, the gunships swept in over the shore line. *(The women run swiftly and smoothly downstage among the bodies, then back upstage. One of the women remains downstage and relates to Speaker 4.)*

Speaker 4

OK, Otsun. Get 'em ready, we're going home. *(The men move into a triangular formation, seated on the floor. See Ground Plan 5. The women lie down and outline the formation.)*

Speaker 13

They waited, looking over their sights, while the gunships chewed up the tree line.

Speaker 6

Then, moving out, they began the long walk back to the boats.

Speaker 11

The tango boats were waiting, motors running, their gun crews nervously looking over their 50's, watching the water line.

Speaker 12

At least in Korea, he could walk off his hill and relax, Mayfield thought.

Speaker 13

Disgusted, he threw his M-16 to his RTO and climbed into the platoon's command boat.

Speaker 14

A few moments later, they were running down the center of the river. (*The men rock in unison from side to side, as though rocked by the boat. They rock side to side four times, then all do random rocking in any direction, come to rest for a beat, then begin rocking in unison again, this time for three repetitions, then another random breakup, then return to rest, then two repetitions, breakup, rest, then one repetition alternating with breakups until "the boat suddenly slowed . . ." The women, lying down, do gentle rocking motions in place.*)

Speaker 10

Stretching out, Mayfield took a cigarette out of his helmet band and looked at it.

Speaker 4

Forty-three years old, and I'm back living on cigarettes and water.

Speaker 7

His troops lay sprawled around him.

Speaker 9

Two or three were already cleaning their weapons.

Speaker 4

Mayfield watched them, realizing without the least satisfaction that if they had to they'd go again and again.

Speaker 6

It wasn't because they wanted to or even believed in what they were doing, but because they were there and someone told them to do it.

Speaker 4

Strange war. Going for something they didn't believe in or for that matter didn't care about, just to make it 365 days and be done with it.

Speaker 8

They'd go, though; even freaked out, they'd go.

Speaker 5

They'd do whatever he told them.

Speaker 6

No flags, no noise, no abuse.

Speaker 8

They just got up and blew themselves to shit because it had to be done.

Speaker 7

But they always let him know somehow that they would rather be left alone; it would be OK if they caught the gooks, but if they didn't, that would be fine too.

Speaker 6

They had no illusions about why they were here.

Speaker 8

There was no need for propaganda.

Speaker 5

Even if there were, these kids wouldn't have bought it.

Speaker 7

Killing toughens you and these kids were there to kill, and they knew it.

Speaker 9

They took their cues from the top, and all that mattered from USARV to the battalion commanders was body counts.

Speaker 4

He'd heard about units of the 101st burying their kills on the way out and digging them up again to be recounted on the way in.

Speaker 7

Just killing made it all very simple . . .

Speaker 9

. . . and the simplicity made it very professional.

47

Speaker 6

The time thing of 365 days just nailed it down.

Speaker 4

To the kids lying around him, Nam simply didn't count for anything in itself. It was something they did between this and that, and they did what they had to do to get through it — no more. (*The men rise and form a column of twos facing stage left. The women rise as well and form a semicircle around the column. Speaker 4 faces the column as though an officer addressing them. See Ground Plan 6.*)

Speaker 12

The boat suddenly slowed, and with the engines easing into a heavy rumbling, the men began picking up their gear.

Speaker 13

A moment later, the boat bumped gently against the hulls of the harbor and, sliding along their sides, came to a stop.

Speaker 14

Mayfield walked over to the railing, sat down.

Speaker 10

The adjutant came up and told him they'd gotten eleven replacements and he could have them all.

Speaker 4

Any lieutenants?

Guitarist

No, just medics and grunts.

Speaker 4

Any ever been here before?

Guitarist

No, all cherries.

Speaker 4

OK.

Speaker 11

Mayfield introduced himself and asked the married kids to raise their hands . . . (*Speakers 11, 12, and 13 reach in, each touch-*

ing one of the men, and sway them gently. The touch may be an embrace. Speakers 10 and 14 reach from a distance.)

Speaker 12

. . . then split them up so they wouldn't be in the same platoon . . .

Speaker 13

. . . he didn't want all the married ones killed at once. *(This is an overlapping sequence, with each woman beginning her repetition when the previous one reaches "married ones," thus leaving "killed at once" to be heard alone on its final repetition.)*

Speaker 12

He didn't want all the married ones killed at once.

Speaker 11

He didn't want all the married ones killed at once.

Speaker 14

He didn't want all the married ones killed at once.

Speaker 10

He didn't want all the married ones killed at once. *(A single staccato percussive guitar chord is played, and all the men turn and face the audience in casual poses.)*

Scene Three: Medics

As the guitarist speaks, the men walk casually to form a large ellipse. The women cluster upstage right. See Ground Plan 7. The moves indicated for Speakers 6 and 7 apply to later speeches as noted below.

Guitarist

At Zama we read in the stateside papers that America was going to hell, that it was almost impossible to get an American teenager to act responsibly, listen to an adult, or, for that matter, even to care. You'd think, then, that it would be impossible to get them to kill themselves for something as vague as duty or run through claymores for anything as subtle as concern. (*One heavy but crisp percussive guitar chord. One by one the women run swiftly to the men. As each woman reaches one of the men, he hits the floor. By the time "killed or wounded" is uttered, all the men except Speaker 1 are down with the women standing over them.*)

Speaker 1

But during the first five hours of Hamburger Hill, fifteen medics were hit, ten were killed. There was not one corpsman left standing. The 101st had to CA in medics from two other companies, and by nine that night, every one of them, too, had been killed or wounded. (*A staccato guitar chord. Speaker 1 hits the floor. Speaker 6 rises and moves to the right of center; see Ground Plan 7. Speakers 10, 11, and 14 approach him. The guitarist puts his guitar down and slowly approaches Speaker 6; when he reaches him the two join hands below the waist.*)

Speaker 10

Pierson, nineteen, was at the rear of his squad when the buried 105 blew. He hit the ground with everyone else, but when the explosion wasn't followed up with small arms fire, he got up and began running toward the settling dust. Three troopers had been blown off the track. One (*Speaker 14 touches the head of Speaker 6 and keeps contact*) had the whole bottom half of his body sheared off; the second (*Speaker 11 touches the head of Speaker 6 and keeps contact*) lay crumpled against a tree, a huge gaping hole in the very center of his chest; the third (*Speaker 10 touches the head of Speaker 6 and keeps contact*), half of his bottom jaw blown off, lay flapping around on the ground, blood gushing out of his neck and spilling into what was left of his mouth. (*The two men raise their joined hands sharply overhead. Speakers 11 and 14 move their hands from the head of Speaker 6 to that of the guitarist. The guitarist is lowered to the floor, bending back until his head touches. Speaker 6 caresses his throat and chest once he reaches the floor, then lifts the guitarist bodily to his feet as Speaker 10 delivers her lines. As the description of the*

50

morphine injection is given, the guitarist becomes the hypodermic needle. Speakers 11, 14, and 6 encircle his body with their arms without touching him, and move down and up as though they were outside of the hypodermic, or as a healing force of some kind. The accuracy of the metaphor is less important than the precision and gentleness of the ritual in dealing with a dying body.)

Speaker 14

Pierson wrestled him quiet. While the rest of the squad hurried by, he took out his knife and, grabbing the protruding piece of jawbone, forced back the soldier's head and calmly cut open his throat, then punched a hole into the windpipe. A sputtering of blood and foam came out through the incision, and as his breathing eased, the soldier quieted.

Speaker 10

Taking an endotracheal tube out of his kit, Pierson slipped it in through the incision and threaded it down into the soldier's lungs, listened for the normal inward and outward hiss of air, then reached for the morphine. Without looking up, Pierson shoved the needle deep into the soldier's arm and drove the plunger smoothly down the barrel of the syringe. (*A sharp staccato cry from all the men. Speaker 6 goes to his knees, the guitarist returns to his place, and the focus shifts to the left end of the ellipse where Speaker 7 rises, facing stage right; see Ground Plan 7. Speakers 10, 12, 13, and 14 move to Speaker 7, kneel on all four sides of him and place their hands on his waist. They set up an undulation in his body which is accompanied by a gradual build-up in the repetition of "running" by the rest of the cast. Speaker 11 approaches him slowly, and at the peak of the crescendo, suddenly places her hands on his chest, stopping the undulation and the sound. She then speaks the line "until it went off" quietly.*)

Speaker 11

Graham was eighteen years old when a tracer round skidded off his flack vest and triggered a grenade in his webbing. He struggled

51

for a moment to pull it off and then, according to the other medic working with him, he jumped out of the aid station, and kept running . . . running . . . running . . .

All

(*sporadic repetition of the word until a rhythm is set up; it grows to a crescendo*) . . . running . . . running . . . running . . .

Speaker 11

. . . until it went off. (*Speaker 7 goes to one knee, all the women squat except Speaker 13. She and Speaker 9 circle the two poles in the ellipse, represented by Speakers 6 and 7, watching each other warily, suspicious at first, but making a game of it. As the "running . . . running" crescendo rises, the guitarist slowly "finds" the beat of the speakers and reaches peak volume with a repetitious pattern of dissonant notes. On the cue "until it went off," there is one short percussive chord.*)

Speaker 13

Watson had been a troublemaker since he was six. He was a bitter, imaginative, hate-filled kid who had been drafted and somehow had survived basic training without ending up in prison. He was assigned to the medics at an evac hospital and then to the field. When he went on line, the hospital personnel gave him a week to be busted and sent back to the States in irons. When I met him he had been up front with his unit for almost five months. He was soft-spoken, but marvelously animated and alert. The old abusiveness was gone; even the adolescent arrogance had disappeared. He was perfectly at ease and open. (*Speaker 13 squats down. Speaker 9 continues to circle, speaking to the audience. His attitude changes as described in the previous speech. He concludes his speech at the right end of the ellipse, between Speaker 6 and the guitarist.*)

Speaker 9

Why not go all out, man? They need me, and I know what I'm doing out there. Hundreds of cases — fucken hundreds. The big-shot dermatologists, they come down once a week. They look at all that rotting skin and shake their heads and leave. Know what we done? We got a mix-master, threw in a couple of quarts of calamine lotion, a few kilograms of Mycolog for the fungus, and figured some tetracycline and penicillin couldn't hurt, just in case there was any bacteria around. Called it jungle mix and bottled it and handed it out. Fucken dermatologists couldn't believe it. Wanted to know where we'd read about it, what medical journal. Sure, I take chances. That's my job — to save lives. (*The women move in on Speaker 9 and surround him, laying their heads on his chest, shoulders, and back as the speech concludes.*)

Speaker 12

On a routine sweep through Tam Key, a squad of the Americal Division was ambushed. Watson was hit twice, both rounds shattered his leg. He kept helping the wounded, dragging himself from soldier to soldier until he was hit in the neck by a third round and paralyzed. (*One slow dissonant chord is strummed. The three medics, Speakers 6, 7, and 9, stand up in the center.*)

Speaker 3

The Army psychiatrists describe it as a matter of roles. The adolescent who becomes a medic begins after a very short time to think of himself as a doctor, not any doctor in particular, but the generalized family doctor, the idealized physician he's always heard about. (*The three medics move to the other men who are lying on the floor, lowering themselves over their bodies ritualistically, as though treating them in battle. The women hover over them.*)

Speaker 10

Medics in the 101st carried M & M candies in their medical kits long before the psychiatrists found it necessary to explain away their actions. They offered them as placebos for their wounded who were too broken for morphine, slipping the sweets between their lips as they whispered to them over the noise of the fighting that it was for the pain. (*One of the women helps Speaker 5 to his feet, then pushes him gently to the center of the stage. She then runs in front of him and intercepts him in the same symbolic wounding used in Scene One. This action should be coordinated with the guitarist's lines which follow.)*

Guitarist

And so it goes, and the gooks know it. They will drop the point, trying not to kill him but to wound him, to get him screaming so they can get the medic too. *(Speaker 6 moves to the body of Speaker 5.)* He'll come. *(Speaker 6 turns suddenly as though hearing someone behind him.)* They know he will. *(Series of staccato guitar chords which continue until the men have formed a kneeling circle about Speaker 6. The women stand just to the outside of the circle. See Ground Plan 8.)*

Scene Four: Final Pathological Diagnosis

The five women move inside the circle of kneeling men and circle around Speaker 6 who is standing facing stage left.

Speaker 11

The chicon mines the VC and NVA use are plastic. They hold ten pounds of explosive charge and three pounds of fragments.

Speaker 13

They can be pressure-detonated, and the explosive charge can be set for whatever pressure is wanted — a tank, a jeep, a truck, or a person. *("Or a person" is underscored with a sharp dissonant guitar chord, quickly muted. The five women suddenly go down to the feet of Speaker 6 and begin gently but rapidly touching and patting him, working their way up his body as the description continues.)*

Speaker 8

This one must have been a pull-release. It blew after he stepped off it — throwing him ten feet into the air.

54

Speaker 5

When the medic finally reached him, his left leg was already gone, and his right leg was shredded up to his thigh.

Speaker 7

The blast had seared through the bottoms of his fatigues, burning his penis and scrotum as well as the lower part of his abdomen and anus.

Speaker 9

The medic gave him morphine and started albumen.

Speaker 2

A Dust Off was called in, which took him to the twenty-seventh surgical hospital (*Speaker 6 turns sharply downstage, still in place; the women continue the patting, caressing action, moving up and down*), where they took off his testicles and penis, explored his abdomen, took out his left kidney and four inches of large bowel, and sewed up his liver.

Speaker 1

After three days at the twenty-seventh (*Speaker 6 makes a sharp turn to stage right, still in place*), he was evacuated to Japan via the Yokota Air Force base. From Yokota he was taken by chopper to the U.S. Army hospital at Camp Zama. (*Speaker 6 makes a sharp turn back to stage left, still in place.*)

Speaker 3

His left leg was removed by a left-hip disarticulation, and his right thumb and left index finger were sutured. There was not enough skin to close his surgical wounds completely, so his stumps were left open. Despite antibiotics, his wounds became infected. (*Speaker 6 begins turning his body without moving his feet, slowly at first, then accelerating. Whichever woman is facing him puts her arms around him and restrains him.*)

Speaker 1

The fourth night in the ward he tried to kill himself. On the sixth day his urinary output began to diminish, and the laboratory began culturing bacteria out of his bloodstream. On the seventh day his fever hit 106 degrees Fahrenheit (*the women begin backing from Speaker 6, continuing the patting, caressing motion as they do so, until they are outside the circle of kneeling men*); he became unconscious, and seven days following his injuries he expired. (*Speaker 6 lies down on his back inside the circle. As he does so, the kneeling men put their heads to the floor.*) His body was then transferred to the morgue at Yokota airbase for shipment back to the continental United States. (*The men all snap to kneeling attention as they say the following line in unison with intense volume and precision.*)

    All the Men

Final pathological diagnosis.

    Speaker 12

(*as the women speak their lines, they turn slowly in place on the edges of the kneeling circle*) One. Death, eight days after stepping on a land mine. (*From the rhythm of this line and the next, the guitarist sets a loud but unobtrusive rhythm of ringing monotone harmonics reminiscent of the bell heard in large department stores, ending with the last entry of the "outline."*)

    Speaker 13

Two. Multiple blast injuries.

    Speaker 14

A. Traumatic amputation of lower extremities, distal right thumb, distal left index finger.

    Speaker 10

B. Blast injury of anus and scrotum.

    Speaker 11

C. Avulsion of testicles.

    Speaker 12

D. Fragment wounds of abdomen.

    Speaker 13

E. Laceration of kidney and liver, transection of left ureter.

    Speaker 14

Three. Focal interstitial myocarditis.

Speaker 10

A. Right heart failure.

Speaker 13

B. Congestion of lungs and liver.

Speaker 11

Four. Patchy acute pneumonitis.

Speaker 14

Five. Gram negative septicemia.

Speaker 12

Six. Surgical procedures.

Speaker 13

A. Hip disarticulation with debridement of stumps, bilateral.

Speaker 14

B. Testicle removal bilaterally.

Speaker 10

C. Exploration of abdomen, suturing of lacerated liver.

Speaker 11

D. Removal of left kidney and ureter.

Speaker 12

E. Multiple blood transfusions.

Speaker 10

External Examination. (*The women stop turning in place and slowly move in on the body as Speaker 10 delivers the description. The movement should be slow and continuous until "left index finger."*) The body is that of a well-developed, well-nourished, though thin, Caucasian male in his late teens or early twenties, showing absence of both lower extremities and extensive blast injuries on the perineum. There is a large eight-inch surgical incision running from the chest wall to the pubis. There is a previous amputation of the distal right thumb and left index finger. . . . (*Total stillness and silence for a long moment until the guitar chord finally breaks it with the introduction to the song. The cast hums the song very gently. On the first line of the song, the kneeling men go to the floor. They remain there for the second*

*line, return to a kneeling position on the third line, and then rise
and move to positions for the next scene on the fourth line. The
humming opens into an "ahhh" on the fifth line as well. The pattern formed is that of a diamond, like a squad on patrol, facing
stage left; see Ground Plan 9 — the position of the women, however, is that to be assumed as noted below. The guitarist plays a
continuing diminished rhythm, the sound of two notes at a half-
step interval tumbling over each other endlessly, to which the men
move in place: something between rock-dancing and mime-walk-
ing, but always remaining in place. The women move among
them, swaying with them, caressing the space about them like
heat, like dust, like some aspect of the environment described.
After a moment, Speaker 12 begins her line.)*

    Cast

(humming, face down)

        Tonight I'm with myself again

(hold)

        I'm talking with my mind

(back to kneeling)

        These last three months we've talked a lot

(rise)

        And found we're in a bind

(move slowly to diamond formation)

        Not that we're different
        We don't think we're unique
        But the answers that we're questioning
        Are those we've heard you speak

Scene Five: Search and Destroy

    Speaker 12

It was 115 degrees in the sun, and what little shade there was
offered no relief. A dull, suffocating dryness hung over the
paddies, making it almost impossible to breathe.

58

Speaker 13

By seven-thirty, the troopers were already covered with a thin, dusty layer of salt. Instead of swallowing their salt pills, they walked along chewing them two or three at a time.

Speaker 14

A few visibly hunched their shoulders against the heat, but there was nothing to be done about it so they kept walking, trying as well as they could to shelter the metal parts of their weapons from the sun.

Speaker 10

The sweet smell of marijuana drifted along with them. (*The guitar rings with a heavy harmonic A. The dance-walk movement freezes. The women move quickly to the point man, Speaker 7, and surround him.*) A little before noon, the point man, plodding along a dusty rise, sweating under his flack vest, stepped on a pressure-detonated 105-mm shell (*the men give an explosive cry and hit the floor*), and for ten meters all around the road lifted itself into the air, shearing off his legs as it blew up around him.

Speaker 11

(*Another ringing harmonic A*) That evening, the company was mortared — two rounds that sent the already exhausted troopers scurrying for shelter. (*The men hiss and turn on their stomachs as rapidly as possible so that they are facing in the opposite direction, stage right, still face down.*)

Speaker 12

After the attack, those who had been resting found it impossible to get back to sleep. (*The women run to the men and go down quickly over their bodies, holding themselves up with arms and legs, hovering over them, moving and undulating sensuously over the men.*) The heat that the sun had poured into the Delta during the day continued to hang over them, covering them like a blanket.

Speaker 13

Despite the darkness, it was still over 90 degrees. The troopers lay on the ground, smoking grass or just looking vacantly up at the empty sky.

Speaker 14

It was the fifth night that week they were hit. (*The men rise and resume their dance-walk facing stage right. The women move carefully among them.*)

Speaker 10

Before breakfast, a patrol was sent out to sweep the area around the nearby village.

Speaker 11

The troopers got up while it was still dark, put on their webbing and flack vests, and without saying a word, went out. (*The men, with one hand, grab the woman nearest them by the arm, not looking at her, and freeze.*)

Speaker 12

All they found were the usual, uncooperative villagers.

Speaker 13

The patrol, against orders, went into the village, searched a few huts, kicked in a door, and left. (*The men release the women, give a loud, staccato cry, and turn in place, all at the same time. They continue the dance-walk in the opposite direction — stage left. The women begin isolating three more of the men, three who have not yet been surrounded. Two women each on two of the men, one woman for the third.*)

Speaker 14

Later that morning, the company began sweeping again. They moved out on line, humping through the gathering heat, chewing salt pills as they had the day before, looking out over the same shimmering landscape.

Speaker 10

A little after ten o'clock, they began moving through a hedge-grove. (*Freeze. The women have completed the isolation of the three men. A ringing harmonic A on the guitar initiates the freeze.*)

Speaker 11

A trooper tripped a wire and detonated a claymore. (*Another hit-the-floor explosion with vocal cry.*)

Speaker 12

It took down three others, killing two right off and leaving the third to die later. (*The men rise and reverse direction once again, now facing stage right.*)

Speaker 14

Before noon, the platoon strung out along a dike had entered a tangled area of burned-over second growth. (*The women begin to drag their hands over the men, simulating vines and branches. The men pull away impatiently; the women move from man to man, slowly progressing to the stage right end.*)

Speaker 3

It wasn't so big that they couldn't have gone around, but the Old Man wanted to kill some gooks, so he sent them through it just in case.

Speaker 10

Disgusted, they moved into it, and for over two hours pushed their way through the steaming shadowy tangle.

Speaker 11

The thick overhead filtered out almost all the sunlight, making it difficult to see, while the matting of vines and bushes held onto the heat, magnifying it until the troopers felt they were moving through a breathless oven.

Speaker 12

The sweat poured off them as they moved cautiously through the suffocating half light.

Speaker 13

At places the growth was so thick that to get through they had to sling their weapons and pull the vines apart with their bare hands.

Speaker 8

Careful, there . . .

Speaker 9

. . . hold it, man . . .

Speaker 7

. . . don't move.

Speaker 14

The vines and thorns caught onto their fatigues and equipment, and they had to stop to tear themselves loose.

Speaker 9

Watch it, Smithy . . .

Speaker 6

. . . hold up, Hank; there, by your foot . . .

Speaker 4

Fuck . . . I'm caught.

Speaker 8

Watch your step, man . . .

Speaker 10

Scratched and bleeding, they pushed on through the tangle.

Speaker 5

Larry, don't move your arm. Don't move, I think I see a wire.

Speaker 7

It's OK, Frey. It's just a vine.

Speaker 9

(*prolonged scream*) Ahhhh. (*Freeze. By this point all the women are kneeling in a semicircle facing stage right around Speaker 9; see Ground Plan 9. They have placed their hands on the floor around his feet, and as he screams they slide their bodies away from the center. The guitar rhythm intensifies.*)

Speaker 4

(*on top of scream*) Don't move! Just don't move. I'm coming.

Speaker 9

Jesus Christ, I'm on one. (*Repeated. Each of these repeated lines is continued until the following line tops it.*)

Speaker 6

Don't lift your foot. Freeze, man, just don't lift it.

Speaker 5

EOD, EOD, forward! EOD forward! (*Repeated. Speaker 4 runs to the front of Speaker 9 and kneels; Speakers 5 and 8 follow and kneel on either side.*)

Speaker 9

That fucken bastard, that fucken bastard. (*Repeated.*)

Speaker 4

It's OK. It's pressure-release. Don't worry, it's not a bouncing betty. Just don't move.

Speaker 5

M-60 carriers, forward! Ammo carriers, forward! (*Repeated. Speakers 6 and 7 run forward and kneel behind Speaker 9 to the right and left.*)

Speaker 13

The EOD slipped off his rucksack, and laying down his weapon got down on his hands and knees, as the troopers came up with the boxes of M-60 ammunition.

Speaker 4

OK, now, just don't move. I'm gonna stack these ammunition cans on the detonator plate. When I tell you, move your foot a bit, but don't lift it up. OK? (*The five men surrounding Speaker 9 hold their hands out, palms down, and slowly lower them to the floor as the guitar, which has been providing underscoring during the previous excitement, plays a steady two-note rhythm which gets louder and louder until the hands reach the floor. Speaker 14's description accompanies this action. Then it stops, there's a pause, and Speaker 4 continues.*)

Speaker 14

The EOD carefully wiped off the steel plate and placed one forty-pound can on the right side of the plate next to the trooper's foot and another on the left side of the plate.

Speaker 4

OK, man. It's OK. Just step off. (*A heavy dissonant chord as the men return to their places and continue the dance-walk. The women surround the final man who has not been rendered symbolically dead.*)

Speaker 10

Three-quarters of the way through the tangle, a trooper brushed against a two-inch vine (*another ringing harmonic A*) and a grenade slung at chest height went off (*another cry, hit-the-floor*), shattering the right side of his head and body. (*The guitar ends on a crisp, quick dissonant chord. The men form a V formation stage left, facing stage right; the women form a straight line facing them from stage right. They all squat. Speaker 7 squats in the center of the V. See Ground Plan 10.*)

Speaker 13

The platoon finally came out onto a small dirt road.

Speaker 14

Shielding their eyes from the sudden glare of sunlight, they dropped their rucksacks and sat down along the slight rise bordering the road, licking the salt off their lips as they waited for the chopper to come in and take out the body. (*A quick but dissonant guitar chord is used here for transition.*)

Speaker 11

They were sitting there strung out along the road, when they spotted a small figure putt-putting toward them. (*Speaker 10 rises and slowly moves forward. Speaker 7 rises and moves slowly to meet her. Speaker 7 circles Speaker 10 slowly one and a half times, ending up behind her.*)

Speaker 12

When the scooter was less than fifty meters away from them, the old man began to slow down.

Speaker 13

The point, a blank-faced kid, picked up his weapon and got slowly to his feet.

Speaker 14

Holding up his hand, he walked wearily into the center of the road and stopped there, waiting.

Speaker 11

The old man slowed to a stop and stared at the trooper, waiting impatiently for him to move.

Speaker 12

He had a small steel container strapped to the back of his Honda.

Speaker 13

The point leveled his weapon at the little man's stomach and, walking around him, motioned for him to open the container. (*Speaker 10 turns around swiftly to face Speaker 7.*)

Speaker 14

The old man hesitated.

Speaker 11

The trooper calmly clicked his M-16 to automatic.

Speaker 12

Holding it with one hand, he carefully opened the container. (*Speaker 7 holds out his hands to Speaker 10.*)

Speaker 7

Hey, the dink's got cokes.

Speaker 14

The point was reaching into the container when the old man grabbed his wrist. (*Speaker 10 grabs Speaker 7's wrists. Speaker 7 pulls his hands down and away.*)

Speaker 7

Hey! What the fuck?

Speaker 10

Fifty cent. Fifty cent!

Speaker 8

The little fucker steals 'em from us and then wants us to pay. (*Speaker 7 holds out his hands again, only to have them slapped by Speaker 10 who raises her hands high over her head and brings them down on Speaker 7's hands. This ritual continues until it is interrupted by the men clapping their hands; see below.*)

Speaker 11

The point reached in again, only to have the old man slap his hand away.

Speaker 7

Watch it, dink.

Speaker 12

The Vietnamese, furious, reached for the container top and slammed it shut.

Speaker 13

From the side of the road there was the metallic click of a round being chambered. (*The men, in unison, clap their hands sharply, once. Speaker 10 turns quickly to face them.*)

Speaker 14

The old man turned on his scooter and kicked at the starter.

Speaker 5

Hold it! (*The men rise slowly and begin to move toward Speaker 10, keeping the V formation. Once around her, they slowly extend their hands to her in the same gesture as Speaker 7 had used. Speaker 10 responds in the same way, but this time, as she brings her hands down, the men all pull back and she continues to the ground.*)

Speaker 11

The Vietnamese, head down, ignoring them all, kicked again at his starter.

Speaker 5

I want a coke.

Speaker 12

Swinging his rifle, he knocked the top off the steel container.

Speaker 13

The Vietnamese spun around and spit at him.

Speaker 14

The trooper brought the weapon smoothly up into the crook of his arm and emptied the magazine into him, cutting him off his scooter, then calmly reached into his webbing, took out another clip, and pushed it into his gun. (*The men slowly squat about Speaker 10's body.*)

Speaker 11
When the chopper came they were standing there drinking the cokes. They sent their own dead home and left the old man sprawled in the middle of the road. (*As the scene transition is made, the men lie down from their squatting position as though sleeping. This is done as a slow guitar chord is played. As a second, higher, slightly more intense chord is played, Speaker 10 rises slowly, stealthily, and delivers her line.*)

Scene Six: Come On! Let's Go!

Speaker 10
Tet is still out there — coiling and uncoiling in the dark . . . the one truly frightening thought that can't quite be put away.

Speaker 14
At dawn, the Australian and New Zealand soldiers fighting in Nam have a complete stand-to. (*As the women speak these lines in a hushed tone, they move carefully among the bodies of the men, stepping over them, crisscrossing, ending outside of them facing out.*)

Speaker 11
They get up while it is still dark and wait out at their perimeters, rounds chambered, until the mists burn off.

Speaker 12
The British had taught them what they learned in Malaysia and the Sudan, from Omduran and Ismalia, that if you're attacked the attack will probably come out of the darkness.

Speaker 13
So they get ready.

All the Men

We don't. (*As they speak in unison, the men all turn over as if annoyed while sleeping. The women turn back in sharply.*)

Speaker 5

Perhaps it is command laziness or just plain American pragmatism of not wanting to be bothered unless there is something to show for it.

Speaker 7

Whatever the reason, we stay asleep, and the dawn for us belongs to the few scattered perimeter guards, the razor wire, and the cooks. (*Speaker 4 rises and begins to move from man to man, beginning with Speaker 9, shaking him several times until "OK, OK, OK!" Then he moves to the other men, kicking the soles of their feet to awaken then. Each begins rising slowly, as though pulling on socks, pants, boots.*)

Speaker 8

Most of the time it works.

Speaker 4

Wake up, come on, James, get your ass moving . . .

Speaker 11

Turning over, James shook off the Sergeant's hand.

Speaker 4

Come on.

Speaker 9

OK, OK, OK!

Speaker 14

He lay there till he was sure the Sergeant had gone and then turning over again, pulled his arm out from under the poncho.

Speaker 10

Holding his hand close to his face, he could barely make out the luminescent dials of his watch.

Speaker 9

Shit!

Speaker 11

He lay there a moment longer and then, shivering, sat up and kicked off his liner.

Speaker 12

He could hear the Sergeant moving around in the dark, waking the other cooks.

Speaker 13

He began lacing up his boots.

Speaker 14

Suddenly there was a noise (*all freeze*), a short distant sound, muffled by the heavy air.

Speaker 10

He froze.

Speaker 11

Now a second, closer this time, more metallic.

Speaker 12

Cautiously James reached across his flack vest for his rifle.

Speaker 6

(*whispered*) It's OK. Just the guards. (*Movement begins again. The men slowly rise and begin moving in a slow circle. The women move into the center and form a convex semicircle facing the audience. The men end in small groups of two or three. See Ground Plan 11. Each group goes through rituals derived from preparation of food — peeling potatoes, rubbing tables, pouring water, etc.*)

Speaker 11

Relaxing, he let go his rifle and finished lacing up his boots.

Speaker 13

Across the perimeter an icy blue flame flickered, hesitated a moment, and then catching, burnt cheerlessly against the firm grayness of the fire base.

Speaker 14

A second one caught near it and then a third.

Speaker 10

Figures like ghosts floated back and forth in front of the flames.

Speaker 11

By the time James reached the mess area all the gas burners had been lit and the Sergeant was already stacking empty crates for the food line.

Speaker 12

A few strips of corrugated aluminum siding stretched over the open burners were being heated for a grill.

Speaker 13

Two troopers, barely visible in the dim light, were filling the 55-gallon cans with water for coffee.

Speaker 4

James, we've got three dozen fresh eggs over there by the ammunition. Mix 'em with the powder.

Speaker 9

Where?

Speaker 4

There, dammit. Over there near the 50's. (*Speaker 9 begins to cross stage right, then turns back.*) Kolstein! Get some more water into those cans.

Speaker 9

Toast?

Speaker 4

Toast what?

Speaker 9

Are we going to have toast?

Speaker 4

Maybe you want some caviar.

Speaker 9

It would be a nice morning for toast . . . OK, forget it. (*Speaker 9 continues on his way.*)

Speaker 11

He took a few steps out over the uneven ground, stopped, and turned around. (*Speaker 9 stops, turns back.*)

70

Speaker 9

Any bacon?

Speaker 4

You getting wise again. I've warned you.

Speaker 12

James shrugged and continued on his way. The eggs were piled behind the 50-caliber ammunition.

Speaker 13

He never found them. (*Everyone screams at once. Each person hits a single pitch and holds it as long as possible. The pitch should not change, and the effect is more sirenlike than human. It should not stop at once, but die away as one voice after another runs out of breath until only a single voice is left. The lights may be raised suddenly to accompany this scream explosion, returning to normal as the voices die out. All the cast members keep their mouths wide open until the final scream dies. As the scream begins, the women move slowly to one or another of the groups of men.*)

Guitarist

The first round hit in the middle of the ammunition. It was the same all over Nam. In the two months of Tet following that morning, 4114 Americans were killed, 19,285 were wounded, and 604 were lost. But on that morning, it was the cooks and the perimeter guards who died first. (*There is a guitar introduction to the song.*)

All

You sent us here to join you —

(*As the whole cast begins to sing the song, it is interrupted brusquely by Speaker 2, who then moves about among the men as though a company commander on inspection, followed by Speaker 3, his sergeant. They move upstage left.*)

Speaker 2

Don't let the news media fool you. These kids may be eighteen or nineteen, but they're beautiful killers — just beautiful.

71

Scene Seven: No Fucken Cornflakes

Speaker 3

There were no more heavily armed night patrols setting up outside the perimeter of the fire base and shooting up anything that came near.

Speaker 2

The gooks would fix their position, set up an ambush, and get them coming back in the morning.

Speaker 3

Then Brigade had tried roving patrols, but the troopers, untrained for night action, got themselves caught and murdered out in the open.

Speaker 2

There was talk about giving up the whole idea and leaving Charlie everything outside the NPD, but the Old Man wouldn't have it. (*The other men approach Speakers 2 and 3 in pairs, salute them, and circle back to form a line stage center from right to left. See Ground Plan 12. When the line is formed, all squat down and begin a ritual suggesting the face-blackening described below.*)

Speaker 3

So they asked for volunteers — eighteen- and nineteen-year-olds — two-man ambush teams who would crawl out at night and bring down anything they could.

Speaker 2

No guns, no webb gear or helmet or even a canteen — nothing that could make any noise and give them away.

Speaker 3

The thing was to go out clean, with only a knife or a bayonet — and maybe a bicycle chain.

Speaker 7

Ready?

Speaker 11

Johnson held the mirror closer as he blackened the last exposed patch of his right cheek.

72

Speaker 12

It was almost dusk; the perimeter guards were already moving out toward the wire.

Speaker 7

Come on, come on. (*Speaker 7 rises and begins moving in a circle at a very slow pace, like a dead march. One by one, the others follow him in the same slow march. As the actions are described there should be no attempt to duplicate the description realistically. The women move in a counter circle outside the men at the same slow pace, freezing when the men do. The language, however, should continue at a normal pace.*)

Speaker 13

Johnson tilted the mirror to take advantage of the fading light for a final check on his face.

Speaker 7

Jesus, man, come on, will you?

Speaker 6

OK, OK.

Speaker 14

Two of the guards, their M-60's casually slung behind their shoulders, stared at them as they passed. Johnson waved to them.

Speaker 7

For Christ's sake, you can wave at the crowd when we get back. (*All freeze.*)

Speaker 10

Johnson walked over to one of the scattered ammunition crates and, resting his foot on it, tightened the bayonet sheath strapped to his leg.

Speaker 11

Straightening up, he shook his foot and stamped on the ground to make sure the bayonet was securely clipped in its scabbard. (*All begin moving again.*)

Speaker 6

The wire. Whose idea was it?

Speaker 7

How the hell should I know?

Speaker 6

It ain't a good idea. It wouldn't keep 'em out, and if they hit us, it's gonna keep us in.

Speaker 7

Well, Mr. Strategist, since we ain't gonna be inside, we don't have to worry about that now, do we?

Speaker 6

It's still a piss-poor idea.

Speaker 7

Tell the Old Man tomorrow, will you?

Speaker 6

What we got? (*Freeze. Speaker 7 raises his arms as though sighting for direction.*)

Speaker 7

Northwest, 180 to 270 degrees. The C and C chopper saw a few of 'em moving in late this afternoon. They lit up a couple. Figured the rest got away. (*All begin moving again. As the circle continues, it gets smaller and smaller until the three teams of two men can touch each other.*)

Speaker 6

Want one?

Speaker 12

Johnson pointed toward the ammunition crate.

Speaker 6

Still some grenades in there.

Speaker 7

Look, man, you know we're not supposed to.

Speaker 6

Sure?

Speaker 7

Listen, wise guy, just because this is your second time . . .

Speaker 6

OK.

Speaker 7

Got your chain?

Speaker 6

Yeah.

Speaker 7

Let's go.

Speaker 13

As they walked across the uneven ground toward the perimeter, Cram scanned the tree line bordering the wire.

Speaker 7

Hold it. (*Freeze. Speaker 7 and one partner in each of the other two teams turn to Speaker 6; the others turn to their partners.*)

Speaker 6

What the hell's burning your ass now?

Speaker 7

That.

Speaker 14

Cram pointed to his companion's shoulder patch. (*Speaker 7 reaches out and touches Speaker 6's arm. The other teams mirror this action.*)

Speaker 6

Oh, for Christ's sake. They can't see it in the dark.

Speaker 7

It's yellow.

Speaker 8

So's the fucken leaves.

Speaker 7

Leaves don't move.

Speaker 6

You win. Just wanted 'em to know who the hell we were.

Speaker 7

They know, man. Just cool it a while, huh? (*Speaker 7 turns*

75

away and continues the circle as do the other teams. From this point the lights dim slowly until the stage is completely black on the cue "began crawling again.")

Speaker 10

They walked on past the last of the tents, toward where the guards were digging in behind the wire.

Speaker 11

About fifty meters from the perimeter they stopped (*all six men stop and turn in place*) and in the dim light carefully checked each other's clothing to make sure nothing could catch or was loose enough to jingle.

Speaker 7

Got it taped?

Speaker 6

Sure.

Speaker 7

Let's see it.

Speaker 6

I told you, it's taped.

Speaker 7

Let's just see it, huh? (*Speaker 6 and the corresponding partner in the other two teams hold their hands over their heads and continue to turn slowly.*)

Speaker 12

Johnson took out his bicycle chain and held it up for Cram to see. Each steel link was covered with strips of black heavy-duty mechanic's tape.

Speaker 6

Satisfied? It's tough, man, don't worry.

Speaker 14

It was almost dark by the time they reached the wire. (*The men get down on their knees facing away from the center, stretch out on the floor, then slowly pull themselves back into a squatting position where, without looking to the side, they lift their right hands and touch the person to their right on the head. This should be timed with the description, concluding with "tapped Johnson playfully on his bush hat," after which they again crawl out from the center as the lights go to blackout.*)

Speaker 11
Cram got down on his belly and crawled under it.

Speaker 12
Johnson followed. The ground was still soft from the rains.

Speaker 13
With the last bit of daylight fading, they crawled single file through the claymores, out past the trip flares and the phosphorous grenades, and into the high grass.

Speaker 14
About 150 meters beyond the last claymore, Cram paused to wait for Johnson, then rolled over on his side, took a ball of twine from his pocket, and looped one end of the twine around his wrist and the other around Johnson's.

Speaker 10
Tying the last knot, he tapped Johnson playfully on his bush hat, rolled back on his stomach, and began crawling again. (*From this point, there should be as little light as possible. Sound should be the only sensory experience. Again, it seems best not to try to duplicate the sound effects described but rather to search for a suggestive metaphor in sound. Snapping fingers, single guitar strings plucked, sharp intake of breath, rubbing the floor gently, and pauses of absolute stillness: these are some of the very simple ideas that may be used to construct the sound score. Each production will arrive at different solutions.*)

Speaker 11
Fifteen minutes later they came to a burned-over second growth of low bushes and grass.

Speaker 6
Here?

Speaker 7

OK.

Speaker 12

They sat up back to back, each taking the 180 degrees in front of him.

Speaker 14

A mortar thudded in the distance.

Speaker 12

A bird screeched.

Speaker 11

A mosquito hummed close by.

Speaker 10

Far away they could hear the sound of automatic fire.

Speaker 11

Cram turned his head. Johnson tensed.

Speaker 12

He had heard it at the same time, off to the right and a little in front of them.

Speaker 13

It was followed by a second noise, a sharp snapping, then another.

Speaker 6

Buffalo?

Speaker 7

No. Let's go.

Speaker 14

Crawling on their stomachs again, they moved off the rise, parallel to the direction of the noise.

Speaker 11

The sounds were getting louder, the crunching, soft, measured beat of men pushing through the jungle.

Speaker 12

Suddenly it was ominously quiet.

Speaker 13

The two boys froze. To their right they heard the sharp metallic click of a round being chambered.

78

Speaker 10

The first gook broke out a little to Cram's left — a dark shape sil-
houetted against the darker night — and as abruptly faded from
view.

Speaker 12

Suddenly another form appeared.

Speaker 13

The figure seemed to hesitate and was about to turn back when
Cram leaped up and got him.

Speaker 14

For a moment, as Cram worked in his knife, it looked as if they
were embracing, then quietly Cram lowered the body to the
ground.

Speaker 10

Johnson was still crouched when the grass next to him parted.

Speaker 11

He saw a foot, and twisting up, swung his bicycle chain in a long
vicious arc.

Speaker 12

The gook was just bringing up his AK when the chain caught
him across the face.

Speaker 13

Even as he fell backwards Johnson was on him, his fingers digging into what was left of the man's face.

Speaker 14

As they thudded to the ground, Johnson reached frantically for
his bayonet and plunged it into the man's neck, knifing again
and again until he could feel the head coming loose in his other
hand. (*At this point, one of the men sets up a rhythm: first he
strikes his bare chest, then he inhales sharply through clenched
teeth, and repeats the pattern. The other men pick it up, repeating it eight times. The last time the inhaling is omitted; instead a long gentle exhaling sigh is heard.*)

Speaker 10

Exhausted, he collapsed beside his victim, gasping for air with his mouth wide open to smother the sound of his labored breathing.

Speaker 11

He pulled his bayonet from the dead man's neck and a gush of blood flowed out with it.

Speaker 12

Johnson stared at his stained fingers; in the dim moonlight the blood looked like quicksilver.

Speaker 13

The tug at his wrist brought him back, and in another moment Cram was beside him.

Speaker 7

Come on. They might be coming back. . . . Hey! Leave it.

Speaker 6

Huh?

Speaker 7

Leave it. The rifle, man. Leave it.

Speaker 6

Nothing doing. This one I'm keeping.

Speaker 7

Why the hell don't you just cut off an ear? Anyway, don't use it, or you'll have the gooks and our whole goddamn division trying to light us up.

Speaker 14

Johnson slung the weapon across his back and, tightening the cinch to hold it firm, followed Cram.

Speaker 10

They crawled for almost a hundred meters before they stopped to rest again and wait for daylight — or more victims. (*The lights come up very slowly. As they do, the men return to their knees, then rise and reverse the circle which we saw before the blackout. In the center, however, we now see one of the women,*

Speaker 13, supine, feet downstage. The officers are seen upstage facing downstage.)

Speaker 11

When it was light enough to see clearly, they started moving back to the base.

Speaker 12

Following Cram, Johnson crawled in under the wire, the same way they had gone out the night before.

Speaker 3

The base was already on the move. All around them troopers were getting ready for their morning sweeps.

Speaker 2

A few stood by their tents.

Speaker 3

Some were filling their canteens . . .

Speaker 2

. . . others fixing their webb gear . . .

Speaker 3

. . . hooking on grenades and smoke bombs or adjusting belts of machine-gun ammunition.

Speaker 7

Hot damn! (*As Speaker 7 yells this loudly, the circle stops suddenly and all turn to him as though startled.*)

Speaker 9

Crazy fuckers. All these ambushers are fucken crazy.

Speaker 8

Got one, huh?

Speaker 7

One apiece. (*The circle recommences.*)

Speaker 9

Come on, I'm hungry. Let's go eat.

Speaker 5

Hey, Thompson, where's Zim?

Speaker 9

The gooks got him. We're going out after breakfast to get him. The Old Man said it would be OK.

Speaker 5

And Cockrane?

Speaker 7

He got back, but he took a round through his shoulder.

Speaker 6

How did it go, Williams?

Speaker 8

A bit heavy.

Speaker 6

Yeah, for us too.

Speaker 4

How did you get it, man?

Speaker 6

Bicycle chain.

Speaker 4

Worked, huh?

Speaker 6

I swear, Truex, he would have had me. I mean I couldn't have got to him without it. You know, I mean he would have blasted me. (*A loud stinging harmonic from the guitar. The circle stops, all the men turn toward the audience, slowly lifting their hands, palms up.*)

Speaker 4

That you? (*referring to the blood on his hands*)

Speaker 6

No, that's him.

Speaker 4

Yeah, I know. I got some of mine on me, too. Took him down from behind. Must have got an artery right off. Jesus! I mean I even got some in my mouth. (*An Fm$_7$ guitar chord is quietly strummed. The men turn back and continue the circle which* *becomes a line as one of the men leads it upstage. See Ground Plan 13. All the men end in a straight line across the back of the stage facing the audience.*)

Speaker 9

Hey, Truex. There's a letter for you in your tent.

Speaker 4

From who?

Speaker 9

Miss America — who the fuck else do you think?

Speaker 4

Wise ass. Hey, Thompson, why don't they ever let us capture some prisoners?

Speaker 5

What the fuck you gonna do with 'em?

Speaker 4

What do you mean?

Speaker 5

What the hell are you gonna do with 'em? Watch 'em all night?

Speaker 4

You don't have to kill 'em to keep 'em quiet. I mean, you can tie 'em up, or keep hitting 'em on the head.

Speaker 5

You keep hitting them on the head.

Speaker 4

I gotta take a piss.

Speaker 5

That fucker's gonna kill me. (*A quick muted guitar chord or harmonic.*)

Speaker 8

How do you figure that?

Speaker 5

He's gonna kill himself and me with him. We went out last night really far; I mean it was really far. He killed one going out — some kid — no weapons, nothing. Probably just from one of the

83

villages. Anyway, the crum got pissed. He wanted an NVA. Stupid fucker. (*During this speech and the rest of Speaker 5's story, he moves out to the body of Speaker 13, not looking at it, but standing over it like a priest. As he does so, the other four women move in slowly, kneel at the body, then rise and slowly circle behind him, changing sides. He lifts his hands over the body as though blessing it, or elevating the host, or some similar image. They kneel again as the story concludes.*)

Speaker 8

Why?

Speaker 5

Motherfucker wants enough NVA belt buckles for a chain. Ever since he killed that NVA three days ago. That's all he talks about, getting that fucken chain. Anyway, that kid he lit up must have been something special to somebody. They were out looking for him all night. Must have been a goddamn company out hunting for him. We laid low. About midnight they were moving back past us. Every fucken one of them had gone by when I swear to god that son of a bitch Truex coughed. I swear to god, that son of a bitch coughed to get some of 'em to come back.

Speaker 6

Did they?

Speaker 5

Fucken A they did, right at us. At least they started. I had some grenades and I just threw 'em as far as I could and got the hell out in a hurry.

Speaker 6

And Truex?

Speaker 5

He sat there like he had a string of claymores. I just cut out on him.

Speaker 8

Maybe you ought to tell the Old Man.

84

Speaker 5

I'm just gonna tell Truex. (*Another quick muted guitar chord or harmonic. A guitar chord concludes the story. Speaker 5 returns to his place, and the whole line of men turns stage left and begins walking in place, the suggestion of a chow line. Speaker 5 remains facing downstage.*)

Speaker 6

What time we going out for Zim?

Speaker 8

I'd thought we'd go out a bit early tonight and get him.

Speaker 6

Yeah, and they'll be waiting for us. Why not now? It shouldn't take long to find him, and with the choppers flying around, the gooks'll be keeping their heads down.

Speaker 7

Oh, shit! They're out of cornflakes. Hey, you! You're out of fucken cornflakes. (*Speaker 3 turns his head.*) Yeah, you, god-dammit! Where the hell are the cornflakes?

Speaker 3

The cook didn't bother to answer. He just turned his thumbs down.

Speaker 7

Fuck it! We work all night; you'd think they'd keep some fucken cornflakes for us. Motherfuckers! Fucken greedy motherfuckers! (*At this point Speaker 2 begins a series of incoherent commands which sound like a drill sergeant counting cadence. As he does so, everyone moves to a new formation; see Ground Plan 14.*)

Scene Eight: Gentlemen, It Works

Speaker 3

Gentlemen, you may smoke. (*All seated men inhale audibly and hold it.*) My name is Colonel Griger, Psychiatric Medical Adviser

85

to the United States Army — Vietnam. (*All seated men exhale.*) This hour of your active-duty orientation has been set aside for a discussion of military psychiatry. I know what is on your minds (*audible inhale*); it is on everyone's mind who is going to war. Let me first try to allay some of your fears. Since you are physicians, it won't be as bad as you think (*audible exhale*). I've just recently returned from Vietnam and I can assure you that your chances of getting hurt or killed — unless you do something foolish or are somewhere you shouldn't be — are much smaller than right out here on the streets of San Antonio, Texas. (*Although Speaker 3 has already been talking in a somewhat ritualistic vein, at this point it becomes a genuine ceremony, the only true religion. Hands raised, turning to the altar, the host elevated.*) Gentlemen, there are achievements that come out of any war; most are truly unimportant and hardly worth a campaign, much less a battle. Others are real advancements, a few major human achievements. Believe it or not — and I know it may be hard to believe — one of these major achievements has come out of the chaos of Nam. It is still controversial, but I believe over the years it will prove itself, not only in the military but in civilian psychiatry as well. Those of us in the military have seen it work already. (*All the men break into cries drawn from the text of the book: "Three VSI!" "Over here! Two burned!" and the like as they move into position, scattered about the stage like the wounded in a corridor. They are spread about in no particular formation, the only necessary placement being Speaker 9 who is just to the right of center. He doesn't move from that point until the end of the scene. See Ground Plan 14. As soon as all reach their positions, the shouting stops.*)

Speaker 4

Major Kohler. The chopper's in. They got some guy who won't move. Says he's paralyzed.

Guitarist

OK. Be right there. (*The women go to the men and trace a pat-*

tern on the floor outlining their bodies.)

Speaker 11

The corridor was filling up with medics and technicians, and the wounded and dying soldiers were already being wheeled past him to the operating room.

Speaker 12

They were carrying them in right off the choppers just as they'd been hit, covered with the mud they'd rolled in, shredded apart, pants legs where their legs had been, filthy tourniquets wrapped around the raw, oozing stumps.

Speaker 13

Some, still in their battle gear, stared up at him wide-eyed, in bewilderment clutching their abdominal packs to their ripped-open stomachs.

Speaker 14

Others, with vacuum bottles swinging from the bottom of their stretchers, had dirty chest tubes stuck clumsily through their skins.

Speaker 10

Several, with bandoliers still slung across their chests, were being piled along one side of the blood-spattered corridor — dead.

Speaker 4

Major Kohler . . . over here. (*The guitarist leaves his stool and approaches the body of Speaker 9. Close by Speaker 9 is Speaker 6, who stands up as the guitarist approaches.*)

Speaker 11

A grunt, with a bandolier of filthy M-60 ammunition over one shoulder, stood leaning against the wall, cradling an M-16 in his arms.

Speaker 12

Kohler was almost up to him before he saw the other soldier huddled on the floor beside the rifleman.

Speaker 13

He had a med-evac tag tied around his neck, but his fatigues were so dirty and cut up it was impossible to tell his rank or unit.

87

Speaker 14

The rifleman came to some semblance of attention, but the trooper on the floor didn't move.

Guitarist

What's wrong? What happened, soldier?

Speaker 6

He come in just like that.

Guitarist

Better take him to the ward. Give him 150 milligrams of thorazine IM and repeat it every hour till he falls asleep, then keep him asleep for at least two days. (*A reverse pattern to that described on page 86 is executed. The men cry the same commands simultaneously and move back to their positions, seated in front of Speaker 3 as though in a classroom, ceasing the cries when their positions are reached. Only Speaker 9 remains in place, and Speaker 2 moves upstage right. The women sit to form a semicircle around the body of Speaker 9, allowing room for the guitarist and Speaker 4 to move around his body. During the cries the guitarist and Speaker 4 begin circling Speaker 9, speaking over the body from the head and feet when discussing him, moving to his side upstage when talking to him.*)

Speaker 10

They kept Dienst sleeping for two and a half days, then stopped his thorazine and let him wake up.

Speaker 11

When Kohler saw him next he was on the neuropsychiatric ward.

Guitarist

Did the neurologist see our boy?

Speaker 4

Yes, sir.

Guitarist

What did they say?

Speaker 4

Nothing wrong, sir. No neurological reason for his paralysis.

88

Guitarist

Good. Now, for the new psychiatry. Sometimes I wish it didn't work so well.

Speaker 13

Dienst was lying on his bed, staring at the ceiling.

Speaker 14

Washed and dressed in a new set of fatigues, he made no move of recognition as Kohler approached.

Guitarist

They tell me you can't move your legs.

Speaker 9

Yes . . . yes, sir.

Guitarist

In the boonies the whole time?

Speaker 9

Yes, sir — except for a week when I got hit and was at the 45th surg.

Guitarist

What happened?

Speaker 9

We got ambushed. I took a piece of a claymore in my hand, sir.

Guitarist

What happened this time? What happened that you got evac'ed this time?

Speaker 9

I don't really know, sir.

Guitarist

Well, what is the last thing you remember?

Speaker 9

The tanks, I guess.

Guitarist

Then? Then?

Speaker 9

I couldn't move, sir.

Guitarist

This ever happen before?

Speaker 9

What?

Guitarist

Your not being able to move — did it ever happen before, at home or at school?

Speaker 9

No. No, sir.

Guitarist

Were you scared?

Speaker 10

Dienst looked confused.

Guitarist

It's OK.

Speaker 9

Yes, sir.

Guitarist

Everyone handles fear and difficult situations in their own way. For some, it's diarrhea; others can't see, some can't move. Your paralysis will pass. We'll talk about it, though, so you'll be able to understand exactly what happened to you. But while we're talking, I expect you to go about your normal duties and to listen to the ward master and corpsman.

Speaker 9

But I . . .

Guitarist

That means everything. The mess hall is down the hallway about twenty meters. That's where the patients in this ward eat. We don't serve food in bed here.

Speaker 9

But . . . but I can't move. I can't move my legs.

Guitarist

Yes, you can, but if you don't want to, you can crawl there. Or

90

go hungry. It doesn't matter to us. Whichever way you want it will be fine. I'll see you tomorrow. (*The guitarist and Speaker 4 circle Speaker 9 slowly. Speaker 4 leaves to join Speaker 2 upstage right; the guitarist returns to his position upstage of Speaker 9.*)

Speaker 14

The next day the ward master called to report that Dienst hadn't moved.

Guitarist

No lunch?

Speaker 4

No, sir, and no breakfast either.

Guitarist

OK; I'll be right down to see him.

Speaker 10

Dienst didn't acknowledge Kohler's greeting. His eyes were sharp and focused, but he still lay staring into space.

Guitarist

You look angry. You're still in the Army, son; I expect you to look at me while I'm talking to you. You must be hungry. I've looked through your 201 file, and you've been a fine soldier. A bit stubborn, maybe. You must have been strong-willed all your life. That's an important thing to be. Not many people are. I know you're hungry. You haven't eaten here, and I know you didn't have time to eat where you came from. Where was it again, now?

Speaker 9

Lang Vei.

Guitarist

I bet you didn't do much complaining there, either. I mean, you're not a complainer.

Speaker 9

No, sir.

91

Guitarist

Tell me what happened out there. Tell me, son. Tell me about the tanks. (*The guitarist kneels beside Speaker 9; the focus shifts to Speaker 3 and his class. It should be evident that this shift and the many others like it are clarified by lighting changes.*)

Speaker 3

Gentlemen, what I want to do now is give you a history of military psychiatry, the theoretical basis for our recent advancement, and why we in the military feel that it works. Freud is dead. He was a great man, but we simply can't use him any more. Let me read to you two quotes from one of his disciples, from a book published in 1957 called *Captain Newman, M.D.* Captain Newman, an Army psychiatrist during World War II, is the chief of a psychiatric service at a large Army hospital. I quote. (*The focus goes stage right where Speaker 2 steps forward. Stylistically it may be useful to play this scene like a sincere but dated TV commentary.*)

Speaker 2

We deal with sickness, the kind of sickness that doesn't show up on sphygmographs or fluoroscopes. A patient may run no fever, or hit 104 out of the blue. Don't think they all babble gibberish; most of them make sense, if you listen to their vocabulary long enough and hard enough. They're using English, but speaking a foreign language — the language of suffering, which requires special symbols. A man can have a pulse that suddenly beats like a trip-hammer or one that doesn't register much more than a corpse's. There's a reason, there's always a reason. To call someone mad is meaningless. There is only one thing you can be absolutely sure of; every, I repeat, every man who's on my ward — no matter what he says or what you hear or what the textbooks say — is sick.

Speaker 3

Now if that's not enough, there's this — I quote from another chapter. (*Speaker 4 steps forward to join Speaker 2. They play*

*the scene as though watching the patient through an observation
window rather than to each other.*)

Speaker 2

What's worrying you?

Speaker 4

Jackson's hallucinating again. He dived under the bed before
breakfast, yelling the Japs are here and he wouldn't come out.
He keeps screaming and shivering and begging to go home.

Speaker 2

Did he get his medication last night?

Speaker 4

Yes, but it's worn off.

Speaker 2

Have you tried to coax him out?

Speaker 4

Nurse Blodgett spent half the morning on the floor.

Speaker 2

A man would be a fool to come out for old frozen puss. Has he
eaten anything?

Speaker 4

No.

Speaker 2

Does he have any special favorites in food?

Speaker 4

Chocolate malts.

Speaker 3

Captain Newman wrinkled his brow.

Speaker 2

OK. You put a nice big chocolate malt and some cookies on the
floor, right near the bed. Let him see you. Tell him he'll hurt
my feelings if he isn't back in his bed when I start morning rounds.

Speaker 3

None of it sounds quite right, does it? A little too occupied with
illness and a bit too sentimental. But during World War II it was

93

the Newmans expressing just those concerns who were running all the military psychiatric services. The Newmans got lost in the flood of military patients and ended up in their concern and confusion by declaring a frightening number of healthy men incapable of military service, to be discharged to the V.A. hospitals nearest their homes. (*The focus shifts to the guitarist and Speaker 9.*)

Guitarist

I know things were tough and you'd been pushing a long time. Believe me, there is an end point to anyone's resources. Some guys decide to surrender, or say fuck it and charge. Some panic and get killed; some even decide to just sit there and get court-martialed. You're too tough for that, though, and too concerned. But let's talk more about you later. I repeat, we don't serve in bed here; this isn't a hotel. When you go back to your unit . . . you're going to have to walk.

Speaker 14

A sudden terrified look swept over Dienst's face.

Guitarist

You'll be able to go back, I know it, and so do you. (*The women slowly move in on Speaker 9, face down on the floor, and place their heads over his. This action is completed by the cue "expectation."*)

Speaker 3

Gentlemen, not only were the Newmans sending these combat neurosis patients home, but they were also losing these same men to their units and ultimately to the war. The Army simply could not tolerate the losses. They wanted these men back to duty. With a little experimentation a few military psychiatrists began to get remarkable results. In its simplest form, their success had to do with expectation. (*All the men give a staccato cry and hit the floor. The women stand up at the same time.*)

Speaker 14

That evening a 122-mm rocket hit in the middle of the grounds.

94

Speaker 10

It landed fifty meters from the operating room, blowing in the door and killing a corpsman and a nurse.

Speaker 11

Everyone waited for a second one.

Speaker 12

All through the rest of the compound, doctors, medics, and patients stopped, waiting for the next rocket.

Speaker 13

Kohler, sitting alone in his office, waited like everyone else. Nothing came.

Speaker 14

Either there had only been one or the others hadn't gone off. (*The women leave Speaker 9 and go to form a line at the stage right end. Speaker 9 begins painfully to move himself with his arms alone at first, gradually acquiring the use of his legs.*)

Speaker 10

Sighing, he went back to work and a few minutes later the phone rang.

Guitarist

Good. Just let him crawl there. I know, he's trying to embarrass us. He's just showing the world how little we understand and how brutal we are. Just let him crawl. He's testing us and himself. The important thing is that he's moving. I don't care what the nursing supervisor thinks. He has to crawl before he can walk. I'll see him in the morning. (*The guitarist walks slowly in a circle upstage of the struggling figure of Speaker 9; he finishes by facing him in profile.*)

Speaker 3

Label a soldier as mentally ill, support that illness, show him that it is what interests you about him, and he will be ill and stay ill. Expectation, gentlemen, expectation. It became obvious that the evacuation of combat neurosis from the front was not a cure — but part of the disease; that it was best to treat these boys as far forward as possible; that their unit identification should be maintained and, above all else, the treatment should always include the unwavering expectation, no matter how appearingly disabling the symptoms, that these boys would be returned to duty as soon as possible. (*Speaker 9 has completed the process begun earlier and is standing erect.*)

Speaker 4

Sir, Dienst is here to see you.

Guitarist

OK.

Speaker 9

I just wanted to thank you, sir. I'm going out this morning. All I wanted to do was say thanks.

Guitarist

You'll do fine. Let me know what happens.

Speaker 9

I will.

Guitarist

Good luck.

Speaker 9

I made it through nine months, I can make it through three more. (*Speaker 9 walks slowly over to the group seated in front of Speaker 3 and sits down among them.*)

Speaker 3

No need for psychiatric contortions; no shock waves; no need to conjure up deep-seated anxieties and conflicts. It is combat exhaustion — instead of something ominous and mysterious. It is, quite simply, just having had too much. And believe me, the casual, yet efficient way it is all handled, the official emphasis on health rather than disease, and the lack of mumbo-jumbo have taken the stigma out of having had too much. To the men, it is just something that happens; and more important, it is something they realize can happen to anyone. It is handled that way and it is presented that way. Gentlemen, it works.

Guitarist

It works, but the war goes on. The new psychiatry has done nothing about that. (*The women walk over to the group seated in front of Speaker 3 and kneel down and embrace the men seated there.*) In Nam the psychiatric patients go back to duty. The men are not lost to the fight, and the terrifying stupidity of war is not allowed to go on crippling forever. At least, that's the official belief. But there is no medical or psychiatric follow-up on the boys after they've returned to duty. No one knows if they are the ones who die in the very next fire fight, who miss the wire stretched out across the tract, or gun down unarmed civilians. Apparently, the Army doesn't seem to want to find out. (*Speaker 2, who remained upstage right, begins a series of incoherent drill sergeant commands while everyone moves to new positions: the men in columns of twos, upstage right headed straight across the back of the stage; the women in a diagonal running from up left center to down left. See Ground Plan 15.*)

Scene Nine: Bosum

Speaker 8, in the down right corner of the column, speaks the opening lines to the rest of the column who are very much at ease. Speaker 2 is at attention facing stage left. At the conclusion of Speaker 8's lines, Speaker 2 bellows out an incoherent version of "Attention!" and the men snap to as he turns to them.

Speaker 8

After six months they promoted our colonel and sent him to Washington. It's not that he's a liar or a bad guy. It's just that he likes this shit. If they listen to him, they're fucken crazy.

Speaker 2

TAAANNNNNNHHAAHHHHHHT!

Speaker 12

The officers who run this war survived World War II.

97

Speaker 13

They remember, as if it were yesterday, what it was to lose a division in an afternoon and then go on to worry about losing an army. (*Speaker 2 moves ominously toward the squatting women.*)

Speaker 14

They are not dishonest officers, nor are they particularly short-sighted or brutal; if anything, they are incredibly sincere and dedicated men (*Speaker 2 turns away from the women, pleased and proud*) who unfortunately are locked into the early 1940's. (*Speaker 2 turns back, angry; moves again toward the women.*)

Speaker 10

For all their professional and at times personal restraint, though, they desperately want to win (*Speaker 2, placated, flashes the V for Victory sign, the one that now means peace, at the women, the audience, and back up to his men*), or at least not to lose, and are always, even within the shifting quagmire of Nam, pushing a bit, trying for a better way.

Speaker 2

(*talking to the audience, he moves back and forth between his men and the women*) Bosum had been trying for quite some time. It was not his first war. He'd been in Burma and Korea. Things had been tougher then, much tougher, but they had never been so confused or muddled. In Nam, he'd been assigned to MACV as an operations adviser to the ARVN's and spent his first five months in country trying to understand what was expected not only of the South Vietnamese Army but the Americans as well. (*He addresses his men directly as though giving a series of commands. They answer as though "sounding off."*) No one seemed to know anything. When he questioned his superiors about how many men they thought they'd need to do the job . . .

Speaker 3

. . . nobody seemed to know . . .

Speaker 1

. . . worse, no one knew exactly what the job was.

Speaker 2

When he asked if the bombings of the north had been effective
. . .

Speaker 8

. . . the field commander said no . . .

Speaker 5

. . . while the Air Force officers said yes.

Speaker 2

When he asked if the recent troop buildup had changed the complexion of the war, the answer was . . .

All the Men

No.

Speaker 2

(*turns back to the women, then to the audience*) When he asked the ARVN commanders about deployments and orders of battle, they just shrugged. He came to realize that despite what was said, the only real United States policy was to send in more and more troops to fight more and more communists. The number of villages pacified, the amount of area held and people won over were simply manufactured data distributed, as necessary, withdrawn, and manufactured again. The only thing everyone agreed on was that they were killing people, but the killing, Bosum realized, wasn't enough. With it had to go the understanding that the killing and terror must go on until the whole thing was over. If Vietnam could not be handled politically, then at least the solution should be found on the battlefield. Tenshut! Forward march! (*As Speaker 2 gives the command, the squad marches across the back of the stage using very short steps. The women move upstage in a group, momentarily getting in the men's path, then retreating downstage. See Ground Plan 16.*) From the MACV he went to military command. He began by inspecting the field units, going on patrol with them. He found the troops universally sloppy.

99

Speaker 8

They smoked on patrol, played radios, and dropped cigarette butts and candy wrappers around ambush sites.

Speaker 6

Some even lit fires at night.

Speaker 5

They fought well when they fought, but they seemed to give no thought to the fighting until the shooting began.

Speaker 7

If there was any moral at all, outside of the mutual concern of a fire fight, it was a moral of time.

Speaker 2

Company halt! Right face! (*The women are now directly downstage of the men. After the "Right face" command, the men are facing the women.*) He had never seen troops so fatalistic. Even at the worst in Burma, when the only thing between the Japanese and India was 15,000 poorly equipped United States and British troops, there was nothing close to the soporific fatalism he found gripping the GI's in Vietnam. Forward march! (*The men march toward the women with the same small but military steps. The women retreat to the up right corner. See Ground Plan 16.*)

Speaker 9

The troops knew that if they made it 365 days without getting killed or wounded they were done.

Speaker 6

It would be over without even having to look back.

Speaker 4

Everything was geared to that departure date — their hopes, their concerns, their plans.

Speaker 8

Friends, if there were any, came next, and then maybe the VC.

Speaker 2

Company halt! It was an impossible way to fight. He could only wonder how the troops did as well as they did. Right face! Half right, march! (*The "Half right, march!" command heads the men toward the women once again. Speaker 2 leads the men this time. When the women do not move, he finally orders them, with a gesture, to move. The women run below the men to the down left area where they form a line facing out, and kneel.*)

Speaker 4

Bosum was up with the 1st Air Cav when they tried to take Hills 837 and 838.

Speaker 5

Two companies tried for three days, and finally, after almost eighty percent casualties, they drove the VC off the hills.

Speaker 2

Company halt! At ease! He stood there in the valley and watched the helicopters come to take the troopers home. Perhaps he was too old-fashioned not to feel a bit foolish to have seen troops fight so hard to get somewhere only to be taken home just when they got there. But this wasn't to be a war for land. He went back to headquarters in Saigon and wrote a factual report on what he had found. (*Speaker 2 marches back and forth in front of the line of women as though dictating to them. The women hold their hands out, wiggle their fingers as though typing, and occasionally return the carriage on their typewriters.*)

Speaker 11

All the units were understrength.

Speaker 12

Platoons that uniformly were to hold forty-seven men ran with thirty.

Speaker 13

Ambushes were poorly arranged and carried out.

Speaker 14

Recon units were not being used effectively.

Speaker 10

Booby traps were not standardized throughout the same unit.

Speaker 11

Body counts were not reliable.

Speaker 12

The report was fully documented and endorsed. (*All the women move as though pulling a report out of the typewriter and reach for Speaker 2 as he moves back up to his men. This motion of reaching pulls them after him and across the stage to down right where they await the next attack.*)

Speaker 2

Again he kept his more subjective thoughts to himself. Column left, march! After almost eleven months in Nam, he was transferred from Military Command to USARV and took over as brigade commander of the 25th division fighting in the Central Highlands. The unit he commanded has been fighting and tracking for almost three weeks. (*As the men march toward them this time, the women circle upstage of them and move around Speaker 2, as though teasing him. See Ground Plan 16.*)

Speaker 7

Four times in those three weeks their recon units had made contact with at least a regiment of the 17th NVA division . . .

Speaker 1

. . . only to lose them again before any significant battle could be pushed.

Speaker 2

Company halt! About face! Bosum watched it all for one week, then ordered that the recon units, after making contact, were not to withdraw but were to stay where they were and harass the enemy. They were to set up ambushes and keep after Charlie until the units they fixed were hit. Half time, march! (*As the men move forward at half time — stepping on every other beat — they begin spreading out so that they actually end up moving directly stage left rather than as a column moving from down right to up left. The women dart through the ranks, throwing up their hands as though playing a game, ending again by teasing Speaker 2.*)

Speaker 8

It was not a very popular order.

Speaker 5

The six-man recon teams were Ranger units, scouts, and trackers, who were always traveling in unfamiliar terrain and were always outmanned.

Speaker 7

They never knew the best places for an ambush, nor, for that matter, the best escape routes.

Speaker 9

Once they committed themselves, they were always running the risk of being cut off and hit themselves.

Speaker 6

In the first two weeks after his order, three teams were caught and wiped out.

Speaker 2

Company halt! About face! He added more men to each unit, giving them more fire power, and turning them into heavily armed recon patrols. Quarter time, march! (*As the men march back toward stage right — this time stepping on every fourth beat — the women once again dart through them without touching them.*)

Speaker 4

In the next week two more got hit.

Speaker 2

He finally put together three recon units, and they worked for two and a half weeks — ate up parts of two North Vietnamese companies, fixed a regiment for the brigade, and got out.

Speaker 8

The mission was an unqualified if unpopular success.

Speaker 5

The recombined unit had taken sixty percent casualties.

Speaker 9

By the end of the week the men were blaming the Colonel for the disaster.

Speaker 7

They had stopped thinking about home.

Speaker 2

Company halt! About face! The ambush procedures were changed. Instead of one platoon taking part, three were assigned. Bosum's orders were that no one was to open fire unless the odds were no more than two to one. Route step, march! (*The men move out slowly, no longer in step, and begin reaching out for the women. The women reach out as well, but neither men nor women focus on anyone — it is as though they are fighting in pitch blackness. When hands are joined, they simply move by each other, like an unstructured do-si-do. The guitar plays the "music" for this "dance" in slow, repetitious, but seemingly random notes. All begin moving toward the center so that the final image is a tightly packed group of bodies, all moving slowly in and out, then unable to move at all so tightly are they packed. Only Speaker 2 is removed from the action.*)

Speaker 8

There was less rest for everyone, but the brigade started getting eighty percent kills.

Speaker 5

They began to hurt Charlie.

Speaker 4

Their own casualties began going up.

Speaker 9

Units that had been running at three-quarters strength began drifting down to under sixty percent.

Speaker 2

Three days after Bosum issued the orders, a patrol was ambushed, and the relieving patrol got pinned down. He committed another company, then two. The fighting spread. Air strikes hovered overhead, but the fighting was too close to get in. Bosum threw in another company, then the reserve. There was no time to get the wounded out; Dust Offs were canceled and told to stand by. Over

104

a thousand men were fighting, most within three or four meters of each other, in jungle so thick you couldn't even see who was firing at you. It went on for hours. Bosum asked Division for reinforcements, and they airlifted in another company. The killing went on through the night. (*The tangle of people slowly begins to separate. One by one, the men and women lie down on the floor, as though dying. All should be down by the cue "Shot them down where they found them," when the guitar also stops.*)

Speaker 9

Whole platoons were wiped out.

Speaker 6

Squads of North Vietnamese were killed where they lay.

Speaker 4

By two in the morning the fighting turned into hundreds of terrifying individual battles.

Speaker 8

Boys killed one another in the dark, shredded apart by automatic fire from no more than a meter away.

Speaker 5

The wounded, lying broken on the ground, whispered hoarsely to passing figures, only to be killed.

Speaker 7

At first light, the Vietnamese began pulling out.

Speaker 9

The orders were for prisoners, but the bitter and exhausted survivors shot them down where they found them. (*Speaker 2 walks among the bodies, stopping in the center to face the audience, at attention, saluting proud, finally executing a left face so he is profiled to the audience.*)

Speaker 2

It had been an expensive victory. Division was a bit concerned about the casualties, but they decided to wait to see what effect these new tactics had on the enemy before they passed judgment. As for himself, Bosum was impressed. For the first time, the area was clear of NVA, not because the communists had decided to move, but because they had to. (*As the following whispered statement builds, the men slowly come to their knees around Speaker 2. Speaker 4 faces him, and as his statement stops the others, he rises, takes Speaker 2 by the shoulders, and kisses him. Speaker 4 releases Speaker 2, steps back, and the women move inside the circle of kneeling men, making sporadic whooshing noises, like slow helicopter blades, as Speaker 2 goes to his knees. The men and women may be in any order, but it is important that Speaker 8 be upstage and off to the center for the next scene which remains in this tableau: Speaker 2 kneeling in the center, the women kneeling around him, and the men kneeling in a circle outside the women; see Ground Plan 17.*)

Speaker 6

The next night . . .

All

(*repeating softly, sporadically*) . . . the next night . . .

Speaker 4

(*topping the others in volume so they cut off*) . . . the next night . . .

Speaker 8

. . . somebody rolled a grenade . . .

Speaker 5

. . . into his tent.

Speaker 7

Bosum died on the ground . . .

Speaker 9

. . . waiting for the Dust Off.

Scene Ten: Me Either

Speaker 8

I'm gonna kill the fucker . . . no, don't say a word; he's dead and that's it.

106

Speaker 5

They'll just send another one.

Speaker 8

I don't care about the next one, man. This is the fucker that's got to go.

Speaker 7

Listen, Cab, it could be trouble.

Speaker 8

Where the fuck do you think this is — paradise? Look around you. You blind or something? What the hell else can they do to us?

Speaker 9

How you gonna do it?

Speaker 8

Shoot the fucker down, man; just shoot 'em down.

Speaker 6

It ain't gonna be easy.

Speaker 8

Look, the RTO calls him down and when he comes down, we light him up. It's that simple. Bamb! Another chopper gone, man, that's all it is.

Speaker 4

What happens when they find him shot to shit with M-16 and M-60 rounds?

Speaker 8

I've got two AK's broken down at the fire base. Next sweep we'll just take them along.

Speaker 5

What about the First Sergeant?

Speaker 8

He's out here, man; he ain't anywhere else. You don't see him sitting in Saigon, getting fat. Don't worry; when that chopper goes down, he ain't gonna be running over to see who's left to save.

Speaker 7

OK. We kill him, but only this one. That's it — no more!

Speaker 1

What about the chopper pilot?

Speaker 8

He's got to go, too.

Speaker 1

Do you know who he is? One of the guys back at the TOC told me MacGreever's flying the Old Man now. He ain't got long till his DEROS.

Speaker 8

That's tough, man, but you can't shoot down half a chopper.

Speaker 4

I ain't for killing MacGreever.

Speaker 9

Me either. He brought us in those 50's that night, man, and he didn't have to do it.

Speaker 4

Count me out. I ain't killing MacGreever just to grease some fucking Lieutenant Colonel.

Speaker 6

Me neither.

Speaker 7

He flew Dust Offs, too.

Speaker 5

Count me out.

Speaker 3

Me too.

Speaker 9

Me either. (*Speaker 2 rises to his feet, becoming the new Lieutenant Colonel, and roars an incoherent command.*)

Speaker 2

AWROOH HAAAH!

All the Men

Shit! (*The guitar beats out its percussive, staccato chords for transition, like the sound of thousands of birds or helicopters taking off.*)

Scene Eleven: Defoliation

From the previous tableau, the cast moves into two parallel lines facing downstage, much as in the opening scenes, only here the two lines represent the jungle on either side of the road which runs between them; see Ground Plan 18. As Speaker 4 begins the speech he moves downstage of the two lines from stage left to stage right. As he does so, the men lie down, one by one, randomly — dying foliage. The women, left without cover, run upstage as the men around them lie down. The men should all be down and the women upstage by the cue: "An AK-47 round is effective up to 1500 meters." By that time, Speaker 4 is at the right end, and walks stage left, this time between the two rows of lying bodies.

Speaker 4

A lot of people are getting fat out of this, the correspondents, the engineers, the so-called consultants. They don't have to be there. Man, they ask for it, and I hope to fuck every one of 'em dies. Let me tell you about that defoliation program. It don't work. No, I mean it. It ain't done a damn thing it was supposed to do. I'll give 'em there are a lot of dead people out there because of it, but not theirs — ours. The whole idea was to prevent ambushes, to clear the area. Some idiot somewhere sold somebody the idea that if the gooks couldn't hide, then they couldn't ambush you, and they bought the idea, I mean really bought it. The trouble with the whole thing is that the VC and NVA use guns in their ambushes instead of bows and arrows. Nobody mentioned that. They don't have to be sitting on top of you to pull off an ambush. An AK-47 round is effective up to 1500 meters. So we'll hit an area, like along a busy road, billions of gallons of that stuff, and pretty soon there's nothing except some dead bushes for fifty or even 300 meters on both sides of where the road or track used to be. So the gooks will start shooting at you from 300 meters away instead of five, only now you're the one that ain't got no place to hide. Ever try running 100 meters or 200? It takes time, and they're firing at you the whole way. And I mean the whole way. (*As he concludes, Speaker 4 is at the left end. There is a sharp, staccato guitar chord. Speaker 3, who is lying furthest right in the upstage line, comes quickly to his feet. Speaker 4 turns as though to face an enemy, and Speaker 3 moves toward him. By the cue "right off the choppers," they are both at the stage left end. They turn, Speaker 3 to the upstage row of bodies, Speaker 4 to the downstage row, and walk back to the stage right end, stepping over the bodies, slowly, ritualistically, as Speaker 3 measuredly lists the diseases, ending by facing one another at the right end on "and no goddam families to have to worry about."*)

Speaker 3

If there is any blessing in being there it is in the shortness of things. There is no wasting away there, no philosophical concern about medical ethics, about pulling out the plugs and turning off the machines. When they die there they die straight out, right off the choppers. It's sort of clean work. No brain tumors to worry about, no chronic renal disease, no endless dialysis, no multiple sclerosis, no leukemics — and no goddam families to have to worry about.

Scene Twelve: I Don't Want to Go Home Alone

As this repetition of the song is sung, the whole cast slowly moves downstage and faces the audience in a line. After they sing "For

110

experience has its function," they return to the image of hospital beds, one row upstage, one row downstage, as in the opening scene, and lie down. Speaker 1 is again stage left. This time one of the women, Speaker 10, relates to him throughout the scene, as though she were a part of his mind, an extension of his mind, sometimes conscious, sometimes unconscious. The other women each kneel at the head of one of the men, cradling their heads.

Cast

You sent us here to join you
And to fight your distant war
We did, but even those who made it home
Carry back a scar

The answer that we question most
Is one we've heard you say,
"You owe it to your country, boy,
It's the American Way"

We haven't decided you're really wrong
For experience has its function
But my mind is at the crossroad
And I can't find the junction

Speaker 1

You can say what you want about the Army and its problems, but I learned this much from going home: the Army treats you better dead than alive. (*Speaker 10 moves to Speaker 1 and touches his head.*) I know, it was my fault. I shouldn't have got involved with taking the body back. But I did.

Speaker 8

It's coming. (*This sentence is whispered sporadically by all the men.*)

Speaker 1

Tell the ward master. How many did they say?

Speaker 3

One VSI and one SI.

Speaker 14

The huge overhead lights were off, leaving only the night lights to flicker feebly across the shiny tiled floor. (*Speaker 1 walks between the two rows to stage right. Speaker 10, walking over the bodies of the lying men, parallels his path.*)

Speaker 10

He walked quietly down the center aisle of the ward, his footsteps echoing lightly ahead of him.

Speaker 11

The beds lining the wall were barely visible, the patients no more than lumps against the frames.

Speaker 12

From the far end of the ward came the faint mechanical hissing of a respirator. (*Speaker 10 intercepts Speaker 1 at the right end. She holds out her hands to him as though she were the thing described.*)

Speaker 13

He stopped a moment near one of the steel arched Stryker frames to listen.

Speaker 14

The machine's slow, regular rhythm was almost soothing.

Speaker 10

How many times he'd heard it before. (*Speaker 1 turns away from Speaker 10 and walks back the aisle.*)

Speaker 11

Someone had said he'd signed more death certificates than any other doctor in Japan.

Speaker 1

Probably right.

Speaker 12

At Kishine, the respirator was the sound of death, not life; in all his time there, he could not think of one patient who had got off the thing.

112

Speaker 1

How's he doing, Sergeant? (*Speaker 1 kneels beside one of the men lying upstage left. Speaker 4 has previously knelt on the other side. Speaker 10 relates to Speaker 1 from behind.*)

Speaker 4

Not too good, sir.

Speaker 1

What's his temperature?

Speaker 4

Hundred and five. It was a hundred and seven before we put him on the cooling blanket.

Speaker 1

Blood cultures growing out anything?

Speaker 4

Yes, sir; the lab called back tonight — Pseudomonas pseudomallei. Major Johnson put him on IV chloromycetin and tetracycline.

Speaker 13

Edwards bent over to look more closely at the restrained body spread-eagled across the frame.

Speaker 14

The air smelled sweet, like a dying orchard.

Speaker 1

When did he come in?

Speaker 10

He peered at the grotesquely crusted body.

Speaker 11

Even the tips of his toes and fingers were charred and oozing; nothing had been spared.

Speaker 4

Four days after you left. Seventy percent second-degree and fifteen percent third.

Speaker 1

I'll check on him later.

Speaker 4

No need, sir, you'll have your hands full. I'll have you called if anything changes. (*Speaker 1 rises and continues to the left end, walking slowly in a small circle when he reaches it.*)

Speaker 12

It was summer outside, and the night was as warm as indoors.

Speaker 13

He cut across the empty, silent field where the red lights of the landing strip flickered softly in the misty dark.

Speaker 14

Far away he heard the muffled, dull thudding of the chopper, and suddenly he felt alone and desperately tired. (*Speaker 10 touches Speaker 1 on the head, then moves in to him, cradles him, and rocks him. Whenever these "inside-the-head" moments occur, it is as though he is asleep, unconscious, or in a trance with eyes closed. At the other end we see Speaker 3. This is an example of necessary lighting separation. Whenever there is an inside-the-head moment, Speaker 1 should be isolated along with the experience itself.*)

Speaker 3

Gentlemen: You have been assembled here at Yokota Air Base to escort these bodies home to the continental United States. Each body in its casket is to have, at all times, a body escort. Escort duty is a privilege as well as an honor. An effort has been made to find an escort whose personal involvement with the deceased or presence with the family of the deceased will be of comfort and aid. Your mission as a body escort is as follows: to make sure that the body is afforded, at all times, the respect due a fallen soldier of the United States Army. Specifically it is as follows: One, to check the tags on the caskets at every point of departure. Two, to insist, if the tags indicate the remains as non-viewable, that the relatives not view the body. Remember that non-viewable means exactly that — non-viewable . . . (*Speaker 1 pulls away from Speaker 10, but she continues to*

114

circle behind him, talking into his head. At the same time, the guitar plays a series of staccato, percussive chords until Ground Plan 19 is formed. It has a resemblance to the narrow corridor in a plane carrying two coffins. The men and women on either side of the bodies are kneeling. Speaker 10 does not continue, of course, until the formation is set and the guitar chords have faded.)

Speaker 10

With the chopper coming nearer — louder — Edwards walked up a slight rise, past a small, dimly lit sign: KISHINE BARRACKS, 109th UNITED STATES ARMY HOSPITAL, United States Army, Japan, Burn Unit. (*Speaker 3 continues, inside the head.*)

Speaker 3

Coastal Airlines loads the bodies on an angle. Be sure that if the body you are escorting is being carried by Coastal Airlines that the caskets are loaded head down: this will keep the embalming fluid in the upper body. If the body is loaded incorrectly, namely, feet down, the embalming fluid will accumulate in the feet and the body may, under appropriate atmospheric conditions, begin to decompose. (*made final with a quiet, sure dissonant chord from the guitar*)

Speaker 11

By the time he reached the evac area, the floodlights were on and the chopper had landed.

Speaker 7

Its crew chief and co-pilot were already in the open hatchway unstrapping the litters from their carrying hooks.

Speaker 9

The choppers usually came in about ten in the morning, but when a bad burn was evac'ed to Japan, they were flown in the same night.

Speaker 5

Burns are a very special kind of wound, and no physician anywhere wants the responsibility of caring for them, not even for a little while.

Speaker 4

For openers, burns look bad and the patients die. (*A heavy dissonant strum of the guitar. Speaker 3 continues, inside the head.*)

Speaker 3

Each of the next of kin as listed in the deceased's 201 file has already been visited by a survivor assistance officer. This was done in person by an officer in uniform from the nearest Army unit. Every effort is made to pick an officer from a similar racial and economic background. These families have already been convinced of the death by either the presentation of personal effects or the relating of an eye-witness report from a member of the deceased's unit. You need not convince the deceased's relatives. (*one staccato, percussive transition chord from the guitar*)

Speaker 8

Sir. Sir? (*Speaker 1 walks to the other end, upstage of the formation, kneels down at the head of the man lying there, and touches his face. The people kneeling on either side of the two bodies all put their heads down except for Speakers 11 and 13. Speaker 10 follows Speaker 1, and as the description of the wound proceeds, she reaches from behind, slowly takes his hands, and presses them to his head.*)

Speaker 1

Call the neurosurgeon.

Speaker 11

The wounded soldier, his head wrapped, was lying unconscious on his back.

Speaker 13

He began to unwrap the gauze from around the patient's head.

Speaker 11

The boy was breathing; other than that, he looked dead.

116

Speaker 13

Edwards pinched his neck, but there was no response.

Speaker 11

As he unwound the gauze it became wet and then blood-soaked.

Speaker 13

Now he was down to the four-by-four surgical pads, and finally to the wound itself.

Speaker 11

Carefully he lifted up the last pack.

Speaker 13

Despite himself, he closed his eyes.

Speaker 5

(*comes up from his head-down position to deliver the speech, then returns*) He's forty-seven percent burned. Took an AK round a little in front of the right eye. Removed the right eye, traversed the left orbit, removing the left eye, and came out near the left temple, apparently blowing out the left side of his head.

Guitarist

(*there is a fingerpicked chord to begin, with the end of the line underscored and accented*) Don't worry, I'll be careful, Bob. Honest, I'll be careful . . . (*This is "inside the head" again. The guitarist represents the doctor's brother — a memory flash-back. In every case, these inside-the-head moments are framed by guitar chords; if the director wishes, the guitarist can use a specific progression or "theme" for all references to Grant. Speaker 1 pulls away from the memory, and from Speaker 10, rises and crosses to the left end where he speaks to the second soldier, Speaker 6. Speaker 10 again follows him.*)

Speaker 1

Send him to neurosurgery. We'll treat his burns up there.

Speaker 12

He walked across to the other wounded trooper.

117

Speaker 1

How do you feel?

Speaker 14

The soldier looked up at him apprehensively.

Speaker 10

The skin on his face had been seared red and all his hair and eyebrows and lashes had been burned away.

Speaker 1

I'm the chief of the burn unit. I'll be your doctor for a while until you get better.

Speaker 14

The burns, red and raw, ran the whole charred length of the boy's body.

Speaker 12

Unconsciously Edwards began adding up the percentages of burned area, tallying them in his mind. (*Speaker 10, upstage of Speaker 1, brushes her hand gently across the face of Speaker 1.*)

Speaker 10

He suddenly realized what he was doing and, for a moment, as he stood there staring at the burns, he looked stricken. (*Speaker 10 removes her hand from Speaker 1's face abruptly.*)

Speaker 1

How did it happen?

Speaker 6

I . . . I was carrying detonators . . . (*Another inside-the-head moment. As the guitar and then the guitarist speak across the space at Speaker 1, Speaker 10 takes his head, rocks it, then takes him in her arms, rocks him, slowly increasing in tempo. The individual talents of Speakers 10 and 1 will determine much of what is done physically. The guitarist is advised not to play during the speech.*)

Guitarist

Dear Bob: We are fighting very hard now. I haven't written Mom

118

and Dad about it. I don't want to worry them. But we are getting hit and badly. I'm the only first lieutenant in the company who hasn't been hit yet. And last week I lost two RTO's. They were standing right next to me. I know what you said about my flack vest, but you haven't been here and you just don't know how hot it can get. On the move, it's just too damn heavy. It's like your complaint about patients demanding penicillin — sometimes you just can't use it. There is, honestly, something very positive about being over here. I can see it in myself and my men. Not the war itself, God knows that's hopeless enough, but what happens to you because of it. Unfortunately you only see one end of it. That's a bit sad, because there are other endings and even middles. A lot of guys get out of here OK, and despite what they say, they're better for it. I can see it in myself. I'm getting older over here in a way that I could never do at home or maybe anywhere. For the first time in my life, everything seems to count. All the fuzziness is gone, all the foolishness. You really see yourself over here. It works on you, grinds you down, makes you better. Got to go. Say Hi to all the guys in the burn unit. Your brother, Grant. *(There is a heavy dissonant chord, clear and ringing. Speaker 1 snaps free of Speaker 10. Return to present reality.)*

    Speaker 1
What?

    Speaker 6
Detonators. I must have taken a round in my rucksack. They just blew up, and then I was on fire. Tried to tear my gear off, but my hands . . .

    Speaker 1
It's all right.

    Speaker 10
He looked at the cover sheet.

    Speaker 12
David Jensen, MOS B11; 1/30 E-2, 4th Division, 20 years old.

Speaker 11

Twenty years old, he thought. (*heavy, "surreal" guitar harmonic*) Grant's age.

Speaker 1

David.

Speaker 6

Yes, sir?

Speaker 1

I'm going to have the corpsman take you to the ward.

Speaker 6

Yes, sir.

Speaker 1

The first thing we're going to do is put you in a whirlpool bath to soak off your bandages and remove what dead skin we can. It's going to hurt.

Speaker 6

Yes, sir.

Speaker 1

If it hurts, just let us know. Is that understood?

Speaker 6

Yes, sir.

Speaker 1

You don't have to call me sir.

Speaker 6

Yes, sir; thank you, sir.

Speaker 1

David, burns look and feel a lot worse than they are. You're going to get better.

Speaker 6

Yes, sir.

Speaker 12

Edwards watched the corpsman wheel the boy out of the evac area and then left the area himself to go to the neurosurgery ward. It was a long walk. (*Fm₇ chord, from the song, for transi-*

tion. Inside the head. Speaker 10 approaches Speaker 1 from behind, and slowly places her arms, crossed, over his chest.)

Speaker 3

Regardless of the branch of service: The emblem of the Infantry, crossed rifles, will be carried on every coffin. The deceased, where the remains are viewable, will be buried in full military uniform. The emblem on his uniform will be that of the service to which he was attached at the time of his death. (*Return to present reality. A series of percussive guitar chords, loud and staccato, during which the men move from the plane-coffins alignment to Ground Plan 20. At the same time Speaker 9 moves to stage left beside Speaker 1. Both face out.*)

Speaker 13

Edwards walked down the corridor to the elevator.

Speaker 14

Leaning wearily against the wall, he pressed the button, and without looking, stepped in even as the door was opening, almost colliding with one of the patients.

Speaker 1

Sorry.

Speaker 9

Excuse me, sir.

Speaker 1

Yes?

Speaker 9

Do you have any relatives in Nam?

Speaker 1

Yes, I do.

Speaker 9

First Air Cav?

Speaker 1

Yes.

Speaker 9

Is his name Grant?

121

Speaker 11

Edwards nodded as the elevator suddenly slowed to a stop.

Speaker 9

Your brother? I thought so. You sort of look like him. I saw him about three weeks ago. There isn't a better platoon leader in the whole cav. But I can tell you this, they were handing him some shit to do, when I saw him. His unit was on their way to getting their ass whipped. (*Here again an introductory harmonic or thematic progression for Grant, fingerpicked. Inside the head. Speaker 10 moves between Speaker 9 and Speaker 1 and using her own head, moves Speaker 1's head toward stage right. Speaker 10 then begins speaking the line softly, Speaker 1 picks it up almost immediately so it is like an echo, or a slight time lag.*)

Speakers 1 and 10

Why don't you go into Tokyo, Grant? You only have a few days for your R and R. You might as well have a good time.

Guitarist

But I want to see what you're doing.

Speaker 1

It's not nice.

Speaker 10

(*repeating*) It's not nice.

Guitarist

And where do you think I've been? I've seen worse — really a lot worse. (*A cold, percussive, muted guitar chord, back to present reality.*)

Speaker 9

Sir?

Speaker 1

Yes, I know. They did get whipped. (*A very faint guitar harmonic is heard. Speaker 9 takes his place in the upstage V formation. The four women kneeling around Speaker 6 take his arms and legs and pull back and forth in a gentle rhythmic motion during the next lines. Speaker 1 circles above Speaker 6 and delivers*

122

the following section at his feet — stage right. Speaker 4 kneels upstage of Speaker 6 and begins running his hands slowly over Speaker 6's body. Speaker 10 kneels at his head and cradles it.)

Speaker 12

When he got back to the burn unit, he found David in the treatment area, already floating full length in one of the whirlpool baths, his head supported on a padded board to keep it above the waterline, the water gently churning about his burned body.

Speaker 13

His IV bottle, hanging from a ceiling hook, was still working.

Speaker 14

A few of the dressings had already soaked off, and the medic was picking them out of the water.

Speaker 10

Edwards took an admissions chart off the wall rack.

Speaker 1

David, we're going to debride you a bit — take off the dead skin. We are going to have to do it every day, a little at a time. That way it won't be as painful. We're going to put you into the whirlpool every day, and all the skin that is loose, or loosening, is going to be removed. If we don't take it off, it just stays and decays, forming a place for bacteria to grow and divide, and you'll just get infected. That's what we want to avoid, because if the burns get infected no new skin will form. It's going to hurt, and I'll give you something for the pain when I think you need it.

Speaker 11

David had been staring up at him the whole time.

Speaker 12

What was left of his lips were clamped tight against the pain of the water churning against his blistered skin.

Speaker 6

Yes, sir. (*Speaker 1 circles upstage and back to the left.*)

Speaker 13

Pieces of dead skin were already floating free.

123

Speaker 14

The corpsman, kneeling down beside the tub, began picking off those pieces that were still attached but had been loosened.

Speaker 4

How long have you been in Nam, David?

Speaker 6

Five . . . five months.

Speaker 10

David watched the corpsman pick a chunk of skin off his chest.

Speaker 4

How do you like the Vietnamese women?

Speaker 6

Don't know. Didn't meet any gooks.

Speaker 4

How come?

Speaker 6

We killed 'em all. (*The guitarist plays two simultaneous ringing harmonic notes, loud and unmuted. All four women pull on Speaker 6's extremities and put their heads back sharply.*)

Speaker 10

Suddenly David let out a scream.

Speaker 11

His eyes clenched tight, the boy was fighting valiantly for control.

Speaker 12

Blood began oozing from the new patch of raw skin on his chest, and Edwards could see the tears rolling down his burned cheeks. (*A series of staccato, percussive transitional guitar chords. Speaker 2 moves to the left of Speaker 1. Both of them face the audience. This is inside the head; Speaker 10 connects them by touching them both from a kneeling position. Speaker 4 takes his place in the V formation.*)

Speaker 2

Cab, Doc. Where you from?

Speaker 1

Japan.

Speaker 2

Oh. Thought so, saw the Fuji patch on your sleeve. Nice place, huh?

Speaker 1

No.

Speaker 2

I heard that Japan was paradise.

Speaker 1

I work in a burn unit.

Speaker 2

Oh, get many burns over there?

Speaker 1

There's a war on. Remember?

Speaker 2

You mean, you get those guys in Japan?

Speaker 1

Yeah. We get those guys . . . (*A tight, clear, definite, dissonant guitar chord, crisp but not muted, possibly an adulteration of Grant's "theme." The men forming the V formation lie down, feet to center, heads to side. Speaker 8 rises, comes down center above the body of Speaker 6. After delivering his lines, Speaker 8 circles to the right below Speaker 6 and back to the left to stand by Speaker 1. The women rise, move upstage, and kneel beside the bodies of the men lying there, as in previous hospital scenes. See Ground Plan 21.*)

Speaker 8

Bob. Bob! Those flights back from the States are tough. I'm sure you haven't caught up with the time change. Why don't you take a sleeping pill and get some rest? (*During this speech and the next two, dissonant variations on a single guitar chord are heard, ending with the chord itself in a heavy strum.*)

Speaker 13

He wrote a Demerol order for David and then went to his room. As tired as he was, though, he couldn't sleep.

Speaker 10

Every time he drifted off, he'd see Grant's tag: "Remains, nonviewable."

Speaker 11

And all that time in the States he thought he could handle it.

Speaker 12

He woke up in the morning exhausted, and went to the ward.

Speaker 13

Johnson was already in the office.

Speaker 8

You know you didn't have to work today — or yesterday, for that matter.

Speaker 1

I know. You want to go on rounds?

Speaker 8

Let's go. (*Speaker 8 moves up the alley upstage center while Speaker 1 circles the body of Speaker 6.*)

Speaker 11

They walked down the ward, stopping at each bed.

Speaker 12

Fifty percent burns. (*As the women deliver the list of burns and burn injuries, the tempo and volume slowly accelerate, slowed only when Speaker 10, who circles ahead of Speaker 1, turns back and speaks her line at him, softly and intensely. As the speakers increase the tempo, the guitarist beats out an unaccelerating tempo on the face of the guitar. It should be throbbing and steady in the beat.*)

Speaker 13

Eighty percent burns.

Speaker 14

Hand burns.

126

Speaker 10

Half-burned.

Speaker 11

Arm burned.

Speaker 12

Seventy percent burned.

Speaker 13

Third-degree.

Speaker 14

First-degree.

Speaker 12

Second-degree.

Speaker 11

Pseudomonas infections.

Speaker 10

Staphylococci infections.

Speaker 13

Split thickness grafts.

Speaker 14

Full thickness grafts.

Speaker 10

Swing flaps.

Speaker 11

Corneal burns.

Speaker 12

Esophageal burns.

Speaker 13

Tracheal burns.

Speaker 14

Contractures.

Speaker 11

Open wounds.

Speaker 12

Closed wounds.

Speaker 10

Congestive heart failure. (*Speaker 8 now circles Speaker 6 while Speaker 1 moves up the alley. Speaker 10 moves ahead of him.*)

Speaker 12

They moved on down the ward.

Speaker 13

On each bed or posted on the wall above the frames were the patches of the units each patient belonged to . . .

Speaker 14

. . . the yellow and black of the 1st Air Cav . . .

Speaker 10

. . . the red and blue eagle of the 101st Airborne . . .

Speaker 11

. . . the 25th Division, the 9th, the big red one of the 1st and the Americal — (*Speaker 10 turns to Speaker 1 from upstage and raises her arms slowly.*)

Speaker 12

There was a 1st Air Cav patch over David's frame. (*A heavy, "surreal" guitar harmonic. Speaker 1 turns sharply downstage. Speaker 8 is now at Speaker 6's head.*)

Speaker 1

Sergeant, I don't care what you think about morale. They're out of the war now, and I want those damn playthings off the walls. That's an order. Off the walls. (*An accent chord from the guitar — heavy and sure, yet clear. Speaker 1 moves down to Speaker 6. Speaker 10 moves down as well and kneels upstage of Speaker 6.*) David, I'm going to stop your IV. You're going to have to start eating. The ward master told me you didn't touch your breakfast.

Speaker 6

Yes, sir.

Speaker 1

Why didn't you eat?

Speaker 6
No one was there to feed me.

Speaker 1
We don't feed you here. You feed yourself. You've got to start using your hands sometime. We can help you grow new skin, stop your infections, graft you — if it comes to that. But it will all be for nothing if you leave here with all your joints tied down by scar tissue. If you don't exercise and keep the scar tissue and new skin over your joints loose and flexible it will tie 'em down like iron. All that new skin and scar that will be forming has a tendency to contract with time. If you don't keep it loose, you'll leave here as much a cripple as if someone had shot off your arms and legs. Your hands aren't that bad, David. We'll start today with them.

Speaker 6
But I can't hold a fork.

Speaker 1
We'll put wooden blocks on them, and as you get used to handling one size, we'll make the blocks smaller. Understood?

Speaker 6
Yes, sir.

Speaker 1
You married, David?

Speaker 6
No.

Speaker 1
Engaged?

Speaker 6
Yes, sir.

Speaker 1
Would you like me to write her for you?

Speaker 6
No, sir, I don't think so.

Speaker 1

All right. I'll check on you later. (*Speakers 1 and 8 circle the body of Speaker 6.*)

Speaker 10

Later that evening, one of David's blood cultures began to grow out Pseudomonas arinosa. (*Speaker 10 summons the other women with a gesture. They all move down to Speaker 6 and take his arms and legs as before.*)

Speaker 11

The bacteriology lab called the ward, and the ward master called Edwards.

Speaker 12

He told the ward master to restart David's IV and put him on 200 mg of polymyxin every four hours.

Speaker 13

The next morning, after rounds, Johnson got him alone. (*Speakers 1 and 8 face each other, right and left, across the body of Speaker 6.*)

Speaker 8

About Jensen's polymyxin. Do you think his kidneys are good enough to handle that big dose?

Speaker 1

What would you suggest?

Speaker 8

You could destroy his kidneys with that much.

Speaker 1

I could save him too.

Speaker 8

If he's going to die, he's going to die.

Speaker 1

I know. That's the great thing I learned from my trip back to America. (*As the anger of Speaker 1 grows in this speech, Speaker 10 rises from her kneeling relationship to Speaker 6,*)

130

approaches Speaker 1, puts her arms around him, and squeezes him. Then releases him abruptly as the speech ends.) His death is expected. It is expected since there are eighty percent burns, and it is expected that eighty percent will become septic. The whole thing is expected. You're supposed to get burned in Nam; you're supposed to get your legs blown off; you're supposed to get your chopper shot down; you're supposed to get killed. It's just not something that happens. It's expected. (*Speaker 8 moves upstage of Speaker 6, kneels, and begins massaging his body. Speaker 1 moves to the stage right end at his feet.*)

Speaker 14
When Edwards came back to the ward, he found David lying on his back, and the corpsman was smearing on sulfamyelon, spreading it over David's charred stomach as if it were butter.

Speaker 6
This stuff stings, Doc.

Speaker 1
I know. It does that sometimes, but it will get better with time. You sort of build up a tolerance to it. The point is that you need it now. It keeps your skin from getting infected and gives the new skin a chance to grow.

Speaker 6
Can't I have something for the stinging?

Speaker 1
No, David, I'm sorry.

Speaker 10
That evening, down in the hospital bacteriology lab, his second blood culture started growing out another patch of pure Pseudomonas. (*The women release Speaker 6's arms and legs, lie down and reach in over the arms and legs instead.*)

Speaker 14
When Edwards came to work up the new admissions the next day, he stopped by to see David.

131

Speaker 6

How does the skin grow back? I mean, where's it gonna come from?

Speaker 1

From you.

Speaker 6

How?

Speaker 1

The skin grows back from the areas around the hair follicles; the new skin grows out from the lining of these follicles. The new skin just keeps growing out of them, creeping over the burned area, until all these little growing areas come together.

Speaker 6

Why am I going to have to be grafted then?

Speaker 1

Sometimes, if the burns are too deep, deep enough to destroy the follicles, then there is no skin to grow back, so we have to graft.

Speaker 6

Where are you going to get the skin for that?

Speaker 1

From your friends, David, from your friends. (*The women move their hands slowly onto Speaker 6's chest and stomach and hold them there, covering him.*)

Speaker 11

That afternoon they took David to the operating room and covered his legs and part of his stomach with cadaver skin.

Speaker 1

What will you do when you get home?

Speaker 6

School, I guess.

Speaker 1

You've got to be more positive than that.

Speaker 6

I was positive before I got burned.

Speaker 1

I'm telling you, you're going to be OK.

Speaker 6

I didn't even see it. I was just walking. I wasn't even point. I swear to God, I didn't even hear it. Can you believe that? I couldn't even goddamn hear it. (*As Speaker 1 circles the body, the women slowly pull their hands off Speaker 6's body.*)

Speaker 12

Within three days the cadaver grafts failed, refused to take, and Edwards had to order it pulled off, like the rest of the dying skin.

Speaker 13

David, lying in the water, saw him as soon as he walked into the treatment room.

Speaker 6

I'm handling it, dammit. Just leave me alone, will you? Just goddamn leave me alone.

Speaker 14

That evening David ignored his presence. (*Speaker 1 stops at the feet of Speaker 6. Speaker 10 kneels upstage of Speaker 6 and relates to him sympathetically as the letter is described, pulling back, looking at Speaker 1 when Speaker 6 says, "I'm not going to make it, am I?"*)

Speaker 1

I saw you with some letters this afternoon. Nice handwriting. Your girl?

Speaker 6

No, my family.

Speaker 1

What did they say?

Speaker 6

It's in the drawer.

Speaker 10

It was a bright letter, careful, measuredly written, filled with support and concern.

Speaker 11

There was a section about Carol, how much she loved David and how happy she was that he was finally out of the fighting.

Speaker 1

Did you answer?

Speaker 6

I didn't know how.

Speaker 1

They know you're burned. It seems to me they're holding up quite well. The least you could do is help them out.

Speaker 6

I've been throwing up all day. I can't keep anything down.

Speaker 1

Yes, I know.

Speaker 6

I'm not going to make it, am I? I know I'm not. That stuff you keep putting into my IV bottle — the only other guys who get it are the ones on respirators. I know. I've checked on the way to the whirlpool. I know.

Speaker 1

I told you about the pain, didn't I? Have I bull-shitted you yet? Look, if you were going to die, I'd let you know. Right? I'd give you the chance to tie things up, understand? Now, dammit, I want you to think of an answer to that letter. I'll be back in the morning and I want an answer. Is that clear?

Speaker 12

Depressed and angry, he left the ward. (*Speaker 1 moves down center in front of Speaker 6 and faces the audience. The men in the V formation come to their knees, their heads on the floor.*)

Speaker 13

Johnson was right, he thought.

Speaker 10

David would die.

Speaker 14

He was probably, all things considered, dead the moment the round hit the rucksack.

Speaker 10

Edwards went back to his room and sat there on the edge of his bed.

Speaker 11

There was really nothing left to do.

Speaker 12

Almost unconsciously he got up and walked wearily over to his desk, pulled open a drawer, and took out a folder that contained a passage he had once read. (*As Speaker 1 delivers the speech, he raises his hands and strikes the air in a slow, rhythmic ritual which increases in intensity until the word "rage." Then it diminishes until the hands hardly move. Speaker 10 is behind him, and holds his head until "rage," then puts her arms over his and helps stop the repetitive ritual. There are any number of things the guitarist can use to melt into this speech — a chord, harmonic, etc.*)

Speaker 1

. . . the dying experience is extremely traumatic to the young adult, to his family and the treating staff. The meaning of dying is appreciated by the young adult, but the reality of personal death is not accepted. He lusts for life, he now has the full emotional capability to sense the personal depth of meaning in death. As he strives for self-sufficiency and for independence, he can appreciate clearly the total passivity and the absolute dependency of the dying experience. The specific emotional reaction of the newly mature young man to the prospect of personal death is RAGE. He feels that life is completely within his grasp so that death above all else is the great ravisher and destroyer. These mature young men who have worked, trained, and striven to reach self-confidence and self-sufficiency now appreciate what they can do and what they can enjoy and that suddenly it will all end. They are so ready to live, to them death is a brutal, personal attack, an unforgivable insult, a totally unacceptable event. (*The men in the V formation lift their heads, still kneeling.*)

Speaker 2

The young physician responds with the normal rage reaction of the young dying adult.

Speaker 4

He sees death as a destroyer that must be fought with every means possible.

Speaker 9

This normal, youthful rage may lead the physician to assault the dying patient with all kinds of treatment procedures in an attempt to keep death away.

Speaker 7

The task of the physician is not to comprehend the incomprehensible . . .

Speaker 8

. . . but to make the natural work of death and the mourning the most meaningful and most productive for the people with which he deals. (*An Fm$_7$ guitar chord. The men in the V formation put their heads back to the floor.*)

Speaker 14

The phone woke him a little past three in the morning.

Speaker 8

Major!

Speaker 1

Yeah.

Speaker 8

Jensen's temperature just spiked to 105.

Speaker 1

OK. I'll be right over. (*The women prepare to lift Speaker 6 by getting into a squatting position and taking hold of his wrists and ankles. Speaker 1 moves stage left to his head. Speaker 8 kneels above Speaker 6 at the point of the V formation.)*

Speaker 10

David was lying on the frame. All the covers were off, and he was trembling.

Speaker 1

David, David. Listen, I'm going to have to put you on a cooling blanket; it's not going to be comfortable, but your temperature . . .

Speaker 6

I can't think of anything.

Speaker 8

He's been confused for the last hour.

Speaker 1

We'd better put in a central venous pressure. How's his urine output?

Speaker 8

Down 60 cc in the last two hours.

Speaker 1

Does he have any blood cross-matched?

Speaker 8

Four units.

Speaker 1

Respirator?

Speaker 8

There's one down in central supply. We can get it any time.

Speaker 6

Doc. You didn't have to come, not all the time.

Speaker 1

I wanted to.

Speaker 6

They told me about your brother and your taking him home. *(The four women holding Speaker 6's wrists and ankles stand up and lift him with a single thrust. Speaker 6 also tries to lift his body as high as possible. He continues to lift and subside gradually, being lowered back to the floor by the cue: "a rather leisurely giving up." Speaker 1 kneels and holds the head of Speaker 6 during this process.*)

Speaker 12

David was about to go on when, gasping, he suddenly bolted upright and, struggling against the restraints, vomited up a great flood of bright red blood. (*Here the guitar begins a steady two-note beat that continues to the very end. It should be a mechanical mimic of a human heart, unerring until the last three notes — played after the body has been lowered and is still, the last three beats being a reflex action, drained of life, with just enough energy for these fading beats, each slower than the last.*)

Speaker 13

Dying in the burn unit is not normally that dramatic.

Speaker 14

There is usually very little blood; burns die inside out, down at the cellular level.

Speaker 12

It is for the most part a kind of gentle going.

Speaker 10

Circulation falls apart, hearts dilate, lungs gradually fill with fluid, and there is always a certain period of confusion.

Speaker 11

But after it, a comfortable time of unconsciousness, where nothing is done and everything — even the last breath — is a rather leisurely giving up. (*The thrust-lift is repeated. Speaker 6 continues to undulate in the air. The men in the V formation, still with their heads on the floor, also do a series of slow undulations during what follows, as though the beating of the heart were being represented. Speaker 1 continues to hold Speaker 6's head. Speaker 10 has moved behind Speaker 1 and places her hands on his back, moving with him as he moves with Speaker 6.*)

Speaker 12

Suddenly, with the blood still welling out of his lipless mouth, David went rigid and, arching backwards, collapsed against the frame.

Speaker 13

Edwards grabbed the suction off the wall and, pulling open David's jaw, began sucking out his mouth, trying to clear the blood and vomit out of his airway.

Speaker 14

The gasping stopped and there was the more comfortable sound of air moving in and out.

Speaker 1

Get the blood. Set up a cut-down tray and get a tracheotomy set.

Speaker 8

The blood is still ice cold.

Speaker 1

Just hang it. Just goddamn hang it . . . David! David!

Speaker 10

He pressed the oxygen mask over the boy's mouth and he could feel the new skin slipping away under the pressure of the mask's rubber edges.

Speaker 1

David! David! Can you hear me? OK, listen, you have a stress ulcer. We might have to operate tonight. You have a lot of blood and stuff in your lungs. I'm going to have to put you on a respirator. It will help you breathe, so I'll have to make a little hole in your windpipe. It won't hurt. It's just to help you breathe. Honest. Just to breathe.

Speaker 11

The corpsman had set up the tracheotomy, and Edwards held the oxygen mask in place while the ward master quickly cleaned David's neck as best he could.

Speaker 12

The noise coming from inside the lungs was getting louder again.

Speaker 13

Even with the oxygen David was having to fight to breathe.

Speaker 1

I'm going to make the hole now.

Speaker 14

Edwards removed the mask. Little bits of skin came away with it.

Speaker 6

Doc, take me home, too . . . please, Doc . . . I don't want to go home alone. (*The four women slowly lower the body of Speaker 6 to the floor, then crouch down beside it. The guitar heartbeat continues, slows down, and finally stops in mid-beat as described earlier. Speaker 1 removes his hands from the head of Speaker 6, and the women rise abruptly. A pause. Then the guitar begins the introduction to the song. As it is sung, the cast rise and move downstage facing the audience. When they reach the line "For experience has its function" they slowly turn back and move to the same positions they had when the audience entered, lying down as the song concludes. The lights on stage fade, the houselights come up. There is no curtain. There is no curtain call. The bodies remain until everyone has left the house.*)

Cast

Tonight I'm with myself again
I'm talking with my mind
These last three months we've talked a lot
And found we're in a bind

Not that we're different
We don't think we're unique
But the answers we're questioning
Are those we've heard you speak

We haven't decided you're wrong
For experience has its function

140

But you've thrown us out here on the backroads
And we're gonna find the junction

(*The last line is repeated until all are lying down. In the arena production, the cast marched out very slowly just as it had marched in at the beginning.*)

Glossary

Glossary of Military and Medical Terms

AK-47 Communist 7.62-mm semiautomatic and fully automatic rifle.

Angel track An armored personnel carrier used as an aid station.

ARVN Army Republic of Vietnam.

Bandoliers Belts of machine-gun ammunition.

Boonies The countryside.

Bouncing betty A mine with two charges: one to propel the explosive charge upward and the other set to explode at about waist level.

Burr holes Surgical holes drilled through the skull so that the brain and its surrounding vessels can be operated on.

CA Combat assault. Term applied to taking troopers into a hot landing zone.

C and C chopper Command and control. The helicopter the unit commander rides and from which he directs the battle.

Cherries Soldiers not yet exposed to combat; hence, virgins.

Chicon mine A Chinese Communist mine. It can be made of plastic.

Chopper Helicopter.

Claymores Anti-personnel mines containing thousands of little steel balls that blow outward, covering an arc of about 120 degrees.

Craniotomy Cutting through the cranium to get to the brain.

DEROS   Date of estimated return from overseas.

Dust Off   Medical evacuation mission by helicopter. The term refers to the great amount of dust thrown up by the rotors as the med evacs come in to land.

Enucleation   Surgical removal of the eye.

EOD   Explosive ordnance disposal.

50   Fifty-caliber machine gun.

Fire base   An artillery battery set up to give fire support to surrounding units.

Gook   Slang for Vietnamese.

Grunt   Originally slang for a Marine fighting in Vietnam, but later applied to any soldier fighting there.

IM   Intramuscular.

IV   Intravenous injection.

M-16   American 5.56-mm infantry rifle.

M-60   American 7.62-mm machine gun.

MACV   Military Assistance Command Vietnam.

Nephrectomy   Surgical removal of a kidney.

NPD   Night perimeter defense.

NVA   North Vietnamese Army.

105   105-mm shell.

122   122-mm rocket.

Point   The lead man in a patrol.

Polymyxin   An antibiotic.

Profile   The medical status of a patient at a given point.

Pseudomonas   Bacillus resistant to most antibiotics.

RTO   Radio telephone operator.

SI   Seriously ill.

Stryker frames   Hospital beds set up so that a patient placed between two large metal arches can be easily turned over.

Tango boat   Armored landing craft mounted with 50-caliber machine guns; also 40-caliber anti-aircraft gun used for direct fire.

Thorazine   A tranquilizer.

TOC   Tactical operation center, usually battalion level and above.

Track   Any vehicle that moves on treads instead of wheels.

201 file   Personnel file containing all the information on a soldier's time in service.

USARV   United States Army Republic Vietnam.

VC   Viet Cong.

Ventricular shunts   Tubes, surgically placed, which drain excessive fluid from the ventricles of the brain.

VSI   Very seriously ill. Army designation for those troopers who may die without immediate and definitive medical care.

About the Authors

H. Wesley Balk, a doctoral graduate of the Yale University Drama School, is an associate professor in the University of Minnesota Department of Theatre Arts and the artistic director of the Center Opera Company of Minnesota. His work with the University Theatre has been largely experimental; one example of it is the dramatization of *365 Days* which is the focus of this book. As the resident stage director of the Center Opera Company, one of the very few experimental opera ensembles in the United States, he has written and directed several innovative operas including "Oedipus and the Sphinx" and "Faust Counter Faust." He has also directed productions for the New York City Opera, the Santa Fe Opera, the New Haven Opera, and the Kansas City Opera.

Dr. Ronald J. Glasser, a graduate of the Johns Hopkins Medical School, is currently a medical research fellow in the Department of Pediatrics at the University of Minnesota Medical School.